Effortless

Transcending the Illusions of Self-Development

PEP

GRATITUDES

Thank you parents, for inviting me into this wonderful world.

Thank you Ari, for navigating it together with me. And your unwavering support.

Thank you everyone I've met here, for your guidance. Even if at times it was through harm.

Thank you life, for writing this book. I needed to read it.

Thank you reader, for giving it your time and dedication.

May it serve you in the best way possible.

The thing that accelerated my healing the most:

No longer telling myself I needed to heal.

The moment I decided: *"If I stay like this forever, that's OK"*, everything began to shift effortlessly.

I started growing faster than ever.

But I'm mostly just watching it, not controlling it.

Table Of Contents

CHAPTER 1
YOUR AUTHENTIC GOALS

This might sound crazy, but hear me out:

The number one reason people don't achieve their goals is because they don't want to.

Somebody says *"I'll quit smoking"* but 2 months later, they smoke again.

Why? The withdrawal period was over.

The reason they smoke again is because they want to.

That doesn't mean they didn't want to quit.

They just wanted to smoke even more.

And that's okay. Nothing wrong with that.

But when you don't admit it to yourself, that's when things get hard.

You get into cycles of pushing yourself, forcing yourself. Just because you think you "should" do it.

If you succeed, you feel burned out and tired. But if you fail, you feel less about yourself.

Wouldn't it be easier if instead you said: *"Right now, I don't want to achieve this thing. I want to achieve it a little. But I want the other thing more."* ?

Then just relax until one day something shifts. And you want to achieve it more than anything else.

That day, with minimal effort, you'll find yourself simply doing what's required. Because you want to.

People often ask me *"How can you be so disciplined and consistent all the time?"*

But the truth is: I'm not. I just stick to doing only things I actually want to do.

"I should be suspicious of what I want."

- Rumi

There are 3 types of goals:

1. The ones we think we have to do.
2. The ones we've been influenced to want.
3. The ones we actually want.

The first category is an illusion.

There is nothing in life you truly have to do.

Every time you tell yourself otherwise, that's a lie.

Obligations only exist in our heads.

Politicians only have as much power as we give them.

Deadlines don't have guns. And to-do lists are just pieces of paper.

There is literally —and I don't use that word lightly— nothing that you have to do.

— *"But...what about breathing, eating or sleeping?"* —

There is nothing that you have to do. You can always choose not to do it.

As long as you can accept the consequences of your choice.

The second category —goals we are influenced to want— tend to keep us stuck in life.

This is the most common type of goal. And it can be a deeply frustrating experience.

For starters, you generally won't achieve these goals (since you don't want to). But you'll likely feel bad about not doing so — because you think you want to.

On the other hand, achieving them wouldn't be so great either:

If you define success based on other people's definitions, it's possible that you'll work hard to achieve it, only to discover at the end that none of it makes you happy.

The more you drop other people's definitions of success, the closer you can get to the core of what you really want.

Of course, it's possible that some of your own dreams would've been the exact same as the ones you were influenced to have.

So how do you know if your dream is based on a standard set by others, or an authentic desire?

If you often hear a voice in your head telling you what you should be doing or how you should be, chances are that voice was originally someone else's.

So if you ever set goals, pay close attention to your inner monologue:

If you hear *"I should"*, you might wanna ignore that idea.

But if you hear *"I'd love to"*, or you feel your chest expanding and a sense of warm joy spreading through your body at the thought of making it happen, that's probably the goal you wanna go for.

Should you get in shape?

No. But you can if you'd like to.

Should you have a specific morning routine?

Not at all. But if you feel like it, there's no harm in trying it out.

Forget what all the gurus say.

You're alive.

For a short time.

Spend it doing what's true to you.

When you care about a dream, it keeps coming back to you over and over.

Maybe in the form of that expansive feeling in your chest I mentioned earlier.

Or a sense of joy about wanting to do the thing for its own sake.

Not for what it would give you. But for the enjoyment of making it happen.

This makes "goal setting" quite a misleading term.

Because if you're doing it authentically, you're not really "setting" goals at all.

The goals already exist.

You're just paying attention and listening for them.

People sometimes wonder *"which goals should I set next?"*

Why, the ones that you already have of course!

—*"But what if I don't have any?"*—

Even better! Then you don't have to achieve them. Much easier.

—*"But then what do I do?"*—

Anything you want to.

As long as you don't try to harm anybody.

It's important to know the difference between what you want, what you need and what you will.

A want is something we feel would be fun to have. Like our life would be a little better for having it.

But when we need something, we feel it must happen at all costs. Like not having it would be a catastrophe. A big lack.

This creates a sense of contraction and rigidity around the desire.

Which unfortunately, tends to guide our behavior in ways that sabotage that very outcome.

Now what's the difference between wanting and willing?

There's no limit to the amount of things we can want.

If you'd ask me *"what would you want to have in life that's not here right now?"*, I could come up with a long list of things that excite me.

I imagine the same might be true for you.

But the question is: Are you willing to have it? To choose it? To welcome every aspect of it wholeheartedly?

If the answer is yes, then great news, my friend: You've got yourself a goal.

It's only when we welcome a goal wholeheartedly that it truly is a goal for us.

When I say *"The #1 reason people don't achieve their goals is because they don't want to"*, that idea tends to rub some people the wrong way:

—*"Aren't there a million more prevalent reasons why goals are not achieved?*

For example: because they were unrealistic, or aimed too high?

Or because the person gave up halfway?"—

The way I see it, none of those reasons are any different.

A goal doesn't just include its outcome. It also includes the way there.

You can look at one of the highest mountains in the world and say *"God, I'd love to see the view from up there!"*.

But let's be honest, does that thought also mean you really wanna climb it?

Maybe the answer for you is yes. But for most people, it'll be no.

Because the sheer amount of training and risk-taking this requires isn't something we want more than to just keep living our lives

So if you write on your list of goals that you want to become a billionaire, the world's number one soccer player or the first pangender octopus to fly to space, then remember:

It's only a goal if you want it wholeheartedly. Including the effort required to get there.

Anything else is just a fun fantasy.

The same is true about giving up halfway.

Sometimes we misjudge or overestimate the effort required to climb a particular mountain. So at some point we decide we don't want to continue.

That doesn't mean we've failed.

It also doesn't mean the climb was a waste.

Because it brought us a little closer to understanding what we want.

Some desires are meant to take us somewhere. Others are there to teach us something.

It's common for self-help books to tell you that you need to have a massive vision.

A goal so big it takes you 10 years to accomplish.

That somehow, thinking just 1 or 2 years in the future would mean selling yourself short.

Now I don't know about you, but the person I was 5 years ago was completely different from who I am today.

And the one I was 10 years ago would barely resemble me —if it weren't for the fact that our bodies looked similar.

But that's just me. Think about how much society has changed. How much those changes have impacted your life.

If a decade ago, you had made a plan for how you'd achieve your 10 year goal, then that plan would contain a list of steps to be taken in a world which no longer exists. By a person who no longer exists either.

Every step you take changes you.

Every dream you achieve reveals new dreams.

And every project you abandon brings you closer to understanding what you want.

So there's no need to plan for world domination.

Find where you want to go right now.

And start walking in that direction.

If you want your goal to become a reality, make sure it's formulated as a SMAR goal.

—*"Wait, don't you mean SMART goal?"*—

No, a SMAR goal.

Specific, Measurable, Achievable-ish and Relevant.

Not time bound.

If you've paid close attention to what we talked about so far, you won't have to worry about the R either.

The goal being "relevant" is already taken care of, by it being relevant to you.

If it wasn't, it would be someone else's goal.

So let's drop the R too.

But you will have to define it in a way that's Specific and Measurable.

Because if it isn't, it won't be Achievable-ish either.

And achieving them is *kinda like one of the main points* of goals, *you know?*

Let's look at an example of a goal that's neither Specific nor Measurable or Achievable:

Many people say their goal is to reach their full potential.

But let me tell you a secret....

There is no such thing as "reaching your full potential".

You have so much potential that you couldn't possibly reach it all.

Did you know you have the potential to become a life-long beggar without limbs? Or to break the world record of public pants-pooping?

Part of adulthood is choosing which of your potentials you want to live out in this lifetime and which ones you'd rather sacrifice for the comfort of clean pants.

A slightly better example:

"Being your best self" is not specific either. And still impossible to measure.

But it is achievable...

You could achieve it by deciding that from hereon, you have achieved it.

If you want to be your best self, skip the goal setting.

Simply declare that right now, you are the best self you could be in this moment.

And that's not even a lie or exaggeration.

I challenge you to try and be a better version of yourself than you are being right now.

You can't.

You can only be better the moment after this one.

Right now, you're the best you can be with the awareness, capacity and experience you currently have.

But let's get back to those SMA goals!

A goal has to be Specific and Measurable to be Achievable-ish.

"Get rich" is neither Specific nor Measurable (unless Rich is the name of your neighbor and you can fetch him by yelling his name over the garden fence)...

But *"Get one million dollars"* is Specific and Measurable. Which also makes it Achievable-ish

"Get rich" is a goal that can have you slaving away for a lifetime.

Never satisfied because your definition of "rich" keeps changing.

But *"Get one million dollars"* is just a tiny bank robbery away.**

**The information provided on the previous paragraph is for general entertainment purposes only and should not be construed as legal advice. Readers should consult with a qualified legal professional for advice regarding their individual circumstances. The act of robbing a bank is considered a serious criminal offense in the majority of jurisdictions and may constitute a felony under applicable laws. It is essential to be aware that engaging in such conduct may result in severe legal consequences, including but not limited to prosecution, imprisonment, and financial penalties. Furthermore, it is important to recognize that the decision to commit unlawful acts, such as a bank robbery, may raise ethical, moral, and societal considerations. Depending on one's religious, philosophical, and political beliefs, there may be additional moral or ethical implications associated with such actions. Readers are strongly advised to refrain from engaging in any illegal activities and to seek guidance from qualified legal professionals regarding the potential legal implications of their actions. That said, should you decide to do it, I wish you the best of luck, a lot of fun, and that you may not harm anyone in the process.

— Why not add a deadline to my goals? Wouldn't it make me achieve them faster?—

If you don't pay attention to how often they're missed, deadlines can definitely give you the illusion of control.

But life doesn't care about deadlines (otherwise they'd be called "lifelines").

Life happens at its own pace.

Things can come up that matter more to you than your goal.

Things that you don't want to brush aside.

But if you prioritize these while you're on a deadline, you'll feel bad for doing so.

Which makes no sense at all. Because you're doing what you want. What matters most to you. And if the goal truly matters, it'll be achieved in due time either way.

Goals move at their own pace too.

Some take time to mature and be understood fully. Others give you a crazy boost of energy. They can make you do things you didn't think yourself capable of.

Some of the goals I set for five years ahead, I ended up achieving in six months. Others I set as a monthly goal but took me years to finish.

If your goal is something you truly want, you won't need a deadline.

All that matters is that you keep tending to the goal.

Which you'll naturally do.

Because you're willing to do so.

You might be eager to enjoy the fruits of your labor a bit faster.

But let me ask you this:

When you pick a fruit before it's ripe, what happens?

For one thing, it never tastes as good as it could have.

But since you already picked it, you also can't put it back and let it ripen again.

So you might as well let it ripen at its own pace.

And enjoy its full taste.

CHAPTER 2
EFFORTLESS ACTION

What are your biggest, wildest dreams?

The things you want, but always seem out of reach?

What if there was a shortcut to achieve those things in just a few weeks?

Well, more often than not, there is.

It starts by asking yourself this:

"If my dream became a reality right now. What would that give me?"

"What would be different about the way I feel, if this dream were real?"

Once you know the answer, the next question is:

"Can I already get that... without having to first achieve this dream?"

If you refrain from a knee-jerk *"no"* response and let the question sink in a bit deeper, the answer is usually yes.

You see, if we dream of living on a tropical beach, that has a reason.

It represents something to us.

We want more comfort. More relaxation. More warmth in our life.

And maybe moving to Bali has to wait another year.

But you can do things today that give you more of those same feelings:

Making more time to relax. Hugging your friends more often. Wearing clothes that make you feel comfy and warm.

And this is true for many of our dreams.

They are projections of our deeper unmet needs.

Traveling could mean wanting to feel more freedom and aliveness.

Money could mean wanting to experience more possibilities, power or wealth.

What if instead of needing a million dollars, you'd focus on feeling more grateful for what you have right now?

Could that make you experience more wealth?

This idea may seem like giving up. But it's not.

You can still achieve your dreams afterwards.

But focusing on this underlying need is, in fact, a better way to get what you truly want.

What if you dreamt of being famous because you craved belonging, acceptance and recognition...

...then, after years of hard work, you actually achieve it, but now you have to deal with a bunch of jealous haters every day?

You'd be worse off than before.

So taking a shortcut —like focusing on self-acceptance and joining communities of people with similar interests— would've been the superior choice.

Please don't dismiss this idea, until you've actually tried it.

What have you got to lose?

Nothing.

But you may as well receive everything you've been longing for.

And much sooner than you expected it.

Acceptance is always the first step.

You can't navigate towards any destination if you don't start from where you are.

So the first step to getting anywhere is finding your feet.

Can you be where you are right now?

Can you look around and see things without added interpretation or story?

Can you accept:

- Yourself?
- Your surroundings?
- The things you have or don't have?

Because no matter how you twist it, those are the things you'll have to work with.

Oddly enough, once you take this first step of acceptance, you'll often find it was the only step required to arrive at your destination.

If there's one thing I hope this book can inspire you to, it's to work *with* yourself. Not against it.

Plans are useless when they're not based in reality.

They lead to all kinds of thoughts that are painful and unnecessary.

- *"If only this or that external thing were gone, I would be achieving my goal right now."*
- *"If only I were like this or like that, it would all be much easier."*

These are neither helpful, nor enjoyable thoughts to have.

And guess what?

If you want to change, the person who has to do the changing is your present self. Not some idealized version of you which you force yourself to live up to.

You wouldn't get frustrated with your dog because it doesn't fly, would you?

So why create frustration with yourself for not having the habits, traits or capabilities you don't have yet?

Look at what you *do* have.

Then see how you can use that to go in the direction you want to go.

The same is true about your environment.

Any change you want to make, is made where you currently are. Not where you wish you were.

When you see reality as it is, you empower yourself to build a life in it.

When you see yourself as you are, you empower yourself to change.

Conversely, when you misrepresent yourself, you disempower others from relating to you (or offering help).

And when your beliefs don't match reality, you stay stuck.

Welcome what is here fully.

And it becomes something you can work with to create the next thing.

The problem, for most people, isn't that they don't know which steps to take to reach their goals.

The internet can provide you with some basic directions in a matter of minutes.

The problem is being too disconnected from the person who has to take them.

When it seems like your goals aren't going anywhere, ask yourself:

"Where am I going? In which direction are my steps taking me?

Am I doing what I know will get me there?

Am I embracing the challenges with curiosity and creativity?

Or just enjoying the story of how hard things are?"

We love hearing about secret methods and complex systems for achieving our dreams.

Because it gives us a convenient explanation for why we're not succeeding.

"Of course! I need to learn this expert's secrets first!"

It's a convincing trick of the mind to keep you consuming rather than creating.

A good enough plan that you stick with will outperform a genius plan that you don't.

Not losing weight?

↻   Are you eating less calories than you burn?

Not finding a partner?

↻   How many new people have you talked to this month?

Not making money?

↻   Are you increasing the amount of in-demand value you're delivering?

When you're not getting results, the reason is either that you're looking at it from too short a timeframe (remember, goals have their own timeline) or that you're not doing the thing.

If you're not doing the thing, then why not?

Most likely, because you don't want to.

In which case, I recommend that you don't.

Some people might argue *"But then I won't achieve my goal!"*

But after being in this field for over a decade, I've come to believe that's not true.

Everyone's always busy achieving their goals.

It's just that we often have very different goals than we tell ourselves.

Find your real goals, and you'll realize you're already on your way there.

Many people say goals are about sacrificing today for a better future.

But I think that logic is completely backwards.

Think of a goal you once achieved.

How long did the satisfaction of that achievement last?

...now how long did it take you to get there?

If hiking a mountain was mostly about seeing the view at the top, we'd pay for ways to skip the hiking altogether.

Goals are the same. They're mostly about the hike. Achieving them is just the cherry on top.

So if you're currently having a tough hike towards your goal, ask yourself:

Why take this path and not a different one?

There are 100 ways to climb the same mountain.

Some are easy. Some are damn near impossible. Some will have you reach the top battered and bruised, barely enjoying the view.

If someone gave you a roadmap and it doesn't feel right or enjoyable to you, it's because their strategies and plans aren't aligned with who you are.

Maybe they're a more experienced hiker. Maybe they're a masochist.

Whatever the reason is:

Since goals are about enjoying the way up, don't go up in a way that doesn't feel right to you.

Go explore and find a path that brings you joy.

Let your curiosity guide you towards other routes.

Doing things because you think you have to is hard every step of the way.

Doing them out of enjoyment, gives you more energy and usually makes you do them better.

CHAPTER 3
INTRINSIC MOTIVATION

Why did the chicken cross the road?

...because it wanted to.

It's wise to avoid motivational content.

Because it tends to be full of falsehoods.

Let's be honest:

You can absolutely *not* do everything you set your mind to.

Even a 3-year old could outargue such statements.

But the good news is: You probably *can* do more than you think.

If instead of getting motivated, you just do it.

Motivational content can give you an enjoyable surge of dopamine.

But it also fills your mind with delusion.

If you're not motivated to do something, then don't do it.

You might think *"I really wanna do it. It's the motivation that I'm missing."*

But that's not true.

You see, if you want to find motivation for something that means you have motivation already.

The motivation is what motivates you to want to motivate yourself.

So to access it, ask yourself:

"Why do I want to feel motivated for this thing?

What about it is so important to me, that I so desperately want to feel motivated?"

You'll either find the answer in the form of motivation.

Or you'll discover that this isn't as important to you as you thought.

Looking for ways to stop procrastinating is procrastination.

Once you become aware you're procrastinating, you no longer are.

You're aware now. You can just go do the thing.

Don't feel like it?

All good. Then don't do the thing.

Now it's no longer procrastination but reprioritization.

CHAPTER 4

PROBLEM? NO PROBLEM.

"God, grant me the serenity to accept the things I cannot change, the courage to change the things I can, and the wisdom to know the difference."

— Reinhold Niebuhr

What if you know what you want... but there's simply no time for it?

It's an illusion.

Everyone in the world has the same amount of time in a day.

What you're dealing with isn't a lack of time.

It's a lack of decisiveness.

Too busy to do what you love? Calendars don't fill up themselves.

Stop saying yes to so many other things.

—"...but what if these other things are important?

What about my work, my family, my friends, having a roof over my head?"—

You're right.

If those things are more important, then it's decided.

Focus on those things. Forget about the others.

More time is made by sacrificing things that matter to you for things that matter more.

Get clear on what matters most.

Go do that, and don't look back.

Remember:

You have the freedom to sacrifice anything in exchange for anything else.

When you choose not to, that's not giving up.

It is doing what you love.

That doesn't mean you won't often end up sacrificing the wrong things and regret it.

But when you do, the regret you feel is fantastic feedback.

If you are unhappy with how you are spending your time, that can mean two things:

    A. The choice you made wasn't your true priority (in which case you can shift again).

B. You are unhappy regardless, and you're projecting that feeling onto your choice (keep reading).

There's no such thing as a distraction.

Only what you choose to put your focus on.

External stimuli can't "distract you".

But you can choose to be distracted.

You might read that and believe I'm blaming you for being distracted.

But that's not what I'm saying here. (Blame is an illusion, as we'll soon learn).

What I'm saying is: You were never distracted to begin with.

Your focus, contrary to popular belief, isn't something you can lose.

It's a spotlight that keeps on shining. At the very least until you die (and who knows what happens after that).

The only thing changing is *what* you shine it *on*.

If you're shining it on something other than what you want to be looking at, just gently bring it back.

If you find yourself continuously drawn back to the thing you believe you're not supposed to focus on, consider the fact that *"supposed to"*, just like blame, is also an illusion.

Can you point out any real tangible evidence that you were *"supposed"* to do anything?

No, such proof doesn't exist.

It may exist in our words, thoughts and stories.

But not in reality.

What you think of as a distraction might simply be what your heart wants to focus on right now.

Every expertise that is a source of income for me today has been the result of a spontaneous diversion. A random curiosity I felt compelled to follow down the rabbit hole.

In retrospect, the dots are easy to connect.

But at the time, they definitely weren't what I was *"supposed"* to focus on.

Pretty much the opposite of that, if you would've asked society.

There's no such thing as a problem. There are only situations.

Actually, scratch that...

There's no such thing as a situation either. There are only happenings.

Life around us is always moving.

And when we fail to notice these movements, we think ourselves to be in a situation.

As if we are in a static pool of water waiting to be moved by us.

But that's not how life operates.

Life is more like an ocean.

Sometimes quiet, sometimes violent. Never not moving.

— *Doesn't an ocean seem like a place where you can run into plenty of problems?*—

Perhaps.

But a problem is only a problem when you imagine your situation to be one.

And a situation's only a situation when you ignore that life keeps moving.

So in tangible reality, there are no problems.

There's only what is happening.

And your possible responses to it.

—But what if you are unable to respond in a way that makes things better for you?—

Then there's no problem either. Because there's nothing to solve.

Only to accept.

As the great Valentine Michael Smith would say:

"Waiting is."

If you are unable to change something, it isn't a problem.

Because the nature of a problem is that something has to change.

If you *are* able to change it, it isn't a problem either.

Just a choice to be made.

Being late to a party isn't a problem. It's what's happening.

As would be being on time.

Being attacked by a bear isn't a problem. It's what's happening.

Sure, you might die. But if so, then there's no problem to be solved anymore.

Or you might survive. In which case, the problem is no longer happening.

Of course, after the bear attack, we're on to the next thing.

New choices to be made.

The most problem-like things I can imagine to happen are intense forms of prolonged suffering.

Like surviving the bear attack but being horribly injured.

Unable to walk. Slowly bleeding to death as you watch the bear devour your best friend.

Maybe even rip your baseball cards collection to shreds for shits and giggles.

That's how bears are.

Not a fun Saturday.

But like every wave in the ocean, it will pass.

Relief might come in the form of help, creativity, divine intervention or death.

But it *will* come.

1. Looking at it from this perspective, there are 2 types of happenings:
2. Those you can respond to (and therefore, aren't a problem).

Those you can't do anything about (and therefore are to be accepted).

When you worry about a problem, it can seem like your worry is caused by the problem.

But the truth is, your problem is caused by the worry.

—Are you saying none of my problems are valid or real?—

No. They are as real as we make them. And being human, we all make them.

Our experience of them will be very real indeed.

I'm only offering you a possibility that might help create less of them.

To shift from reacting to life with a *"But, no..."*

To reacting with a playful *"Yes, and..."*

Because life won't listen to your butts or your nose.

Just like I won't listen to anyone asking me to correct the typos in the previous sentence.

It will keep happening anyway.

But what life does allow you, is to play with it.

It allows you to add more life to the life already here.

It allows you to say:

"Yes, life ...and now I do THIS.

YOUR TURN."

When you start to see life as an endless stream of happenings which you can participate in and play with, something changes.

Everything becomes more fun and beautiful. Including the parts that are painful.

The pain doesn't disappear. It becomes part of it.

The problem with seeing life as a problem is that it disempowers you.

It all goes back to that first step: acceptance.

When you tell life to be different, you are rejecting the only thing that exists.

But meanwhile, it continues to be.

It's like playing basketball but complaining that the ball should bounce differently.

It won't.

When life starts to feel like a problem, the best move is going towards it.

To be with the ball it passed you. To study its movements. And learn to move *with* it.

Because no amount of cursing the ball is going to make it move in your favor.

CHAPTER 5

CHANGING YOURSELF

"You are under no obligation to be the same person you were 5 minutes ago."

— Alan Watts

You are not your job.

You are not your past.

You are not your body.

You are not your culture or your trauma.

You are not your feelings, your opinions or your behavior.

You are not your potential, your ethnicity, nor the total of your passing thoughts.

What we think is our personality is just a set of behaviors we're accustomed to.

It's perfectly possible to change them at any point.

If you ever hear yourself saying: *"I wish I could XYZ but...I'm just too ABC"*

Then let this be a reminder that "ABC" is not what you *are*. It's how you're *behaving*.

You're free to behave differently —or the same— in each new moment.

Creating change in yourself is as easy or hard as the grip you hold on the things you identify with. All you have to do is something different than you did a minute ago.

But to make the choice to change, you must first be who you are right now.

Because anybody you're pretending to be doesn't really exist.

And people who don't exist —by virtue of not existing— are incapable of change.

Anyway, I just fact-checked this and it turns out that you, dear reader, definitely *do* exist.

That means you have the power to change your personality at any point.

Once you can loosen your grip on the behaviors and beliefs you *think* are you (something we'll focus on in the final chapters of this book), you'll find a freedom unlike anything you've ever known.

The challenge is that when you think this personality is the real you, it feels like letting go of it would be the end of your existence.

But on the contrary....

It could lead to your very discovery of it.

Being the best version of yourself —a lofty goal that has allured many millennials— is not a destination to be reached but a reality to be discovered.

Each new moment, you have the opportunity to check in:

"What's the best person I have the capacity to be right now?"

You might notice that the word *"best"* doesn't actually mean anything without a context.

The best at *what*?

The implicit context we have for *"best"* is often set by other people:

Parents and teachers instilled their ideas of what's good and bad behavior as we grew up.

Religious leaders (including atheistic ones) spread their values across our societies.

Influencers share their wounded definitions of what a *"real man"* or *"real woman" "should"* be like and mask it as science.

Be careful of adopting such contexts. They can disconnect you from yourself.

A cat doesn't need a manual on how to be a cat.

Feel *what you are* in each moment and just be that.

Truth is: That's what you'll be anyway.

You'll either behave to the best of your unconscious ability, or you'll consciously make choices with the most awareness you can muster up right now.

(And if you look closely, you'll see both options are the exact same thing).

What makes it so hard to be your best self is not being it.

It's telling yourself you *could* or *should* do something else than what's happening right now.

Imagine you're in a relationship where your partner always says that you should be different.

Would you feel loved?

Exactly. Let's not do that to ourselves either.

In fact, many of the traits we consider bad or undesirable are the exact ones which arise when we are feeling unloved or unsafe. So criticism is what teases them out.

And loving ourselves —warts and all— can make them disappear (with the caveat that this doesn't work if you try to love them with the intention of making them disappear, for obvious reasons).

Welcome your feelings. Welcome your current way of being. And if you don't want to, welcome that too. Welcome the part of you that's telling you to be something other than you are. Have them all join the party.

That's you behaving to the best of your ability at this moment.

Minus the illusionary struggle that makes it seem different.

There's no way around it.

You are what you are.

That doesn't mean there's no opportunities for growth.

But here's the thing: When an opportunity for growth enters your awareness and you respond with a desire to seize it, then growth is already happening. Effortlessly. All it needs is just a little patience. (♫)

—But what if the opportunity for growth is not met with the intention to seize it?—

Then we're back at the starting premise of this book:

If you're not changing, change isn't what you want (or at least not yet/not in this form).

Embrace that. Embrace yourself as you currently are.

Because that's the truth of your desire.

You can become who you want to be.

Or who you want to be can become who you are.

CHAPTER 6
THE IMPOSTER IS NOT A SYNDROME

If you found some great expert advice but it just doesn't feel quite right in your system, don't force it. Don't impose it on yourself.

Trust your bodily response.

There is another way.

It might take a little longer to find it.

But is a shortcut really worth your soul?

"Fake it till you make it" is terrible advice:

1. You'll feel like a fraud (not great for your confidence).

2. You'll actually be a fraud (not great for your reputation).

3. Most people will know it and they won't tell you.

4. Faking it doesn't actually help you make it in any way. If anything, it makes it harder. Because you can't ask for advice or feedback anymore when you pretend to already be there.

Many so-called cases of "imposter syndrome" are actually persona fatigue.

Imposter syndrome is when you're being authentic but doubt your competence despite there being evidence for it.

Persona fatigue is when your true self is tired of keeping up the facade and wants you to be authentic.

Imposter syndrome happens when you place too much importance on looking a certain way.

Whether you actually are good at something or not is irrelevant to the imposter.

The fear only comes up when we wouldn't want people to think we're anything less than what we're portraying ourselves to be.

The way out is to simply portray yourself as you are in each moment, with no regard for consistency in your image.

What's great about this is that it makes your life a lot easier too.

You no longer have to think about how you want to present yourself.

You can just show up.

CHAPTER 7
CONFIDENT INADEQUACY

—*"But what if I'm not good enough?"*—

Not good enough for what?

You're here.

You successfully managed to stay alive until this very day.

The truth is that you *are* good enough.

Perhaps not good enough to live up to some unrealistic standard of perfectionism.

But definitely good enough for this world.

Otherwise you would be dead by now.

So if that thought comes up, it doesn't mean you *are* inadequate.

It only means that at that moment, you *feel* inadequate.

One of the main reasons feelings of inadequacy persist is that we continue to search for a way to fix them.

As with many things, the doorway out of our perceived problems is seeing the circular logic that's creating them. And doing our best to laugh a little more than we cry about it.

Each time you search for a solution to inadequacy, you reinforce the (usually false) idea that there is something wrong with you which needs fixing.

In other words: trying to fix yourself is what makes you think you need to.

People who sell "solutions" to this problem know that.

They will draw you in with well-chosen words that put you in touch with your deepest insecurities.

Then they'll make you believe you finally found the root of the issue, but it's just out of reach.

Finally they'll hit you with the finisher:

"You can take this supplement, wear these clothes, or join my sacred autofellatio retreat in the Himalaya mountains.

It's valued at $4,586,869. But there's only 2 spots available.

So if you pay within 30 minutes I'll give it to you for a meager $11,011 instead.

Don't worry child, I will fix you!"

Some of these people might even believe they're telling you the truth!

When we try an expensive service or product meant to improve us in some way, our faith in it can make us feel "fixed" for a while.

Until suddenly one day, the very normal feeling of inadequacy pops up again.

Now the mind might think:

"Wait a minute? It worked for everyone else, yet I don't seem to be fully fixed.

There must be something wrong with me on a deeper level."

This restarts the cycle with a little bit more anxiety and a little bit more willingness to dish out larger amounts of money for the next "cure".

If for some reason, a product or service were to convince us that because of using it, we're completely healed, then that would be an unhelpful belief too.

A mask in front of the mirror. A bandage to cover the wound but not heal it.

Because having an external "fix" to rely on solidifies the belief that we are not good enough without it. Otherwise, why would we need the fix?

When we're in that situation, it may not always be obvious.

As the belief will be covered up with the illusion of confidence.

But underneath, the feelings are still there, growing stronger.

The subtle distinction is:

There's confidence in the supplements, confidence in the million dollar morning routine or confidence in the rare esoteric manifestation technique™. But not in the person who's doing it.

What if you forget your pills? What if the manifestation practice was made impossible for an entire month? Then the person would be "inadequate" again!

Oh no!

"Better do the thing every day. Preferably at 4AM because that's how adequate people do it."

Once you become aware of this, you may conclude that the product or service didn't help at all.

And on some level, that's true.

The only question is:

Will you conclude it couldn't fix you because you are "broken"?

Or that it couldn't fix you because you are already whole?

Life is like a series of infinite loops.

The same situation will happen to us over and over in different forms.

Sometimes for decades.

Until we finally face the nature of the loop.

Until we realize once again that we are the one perpetually recreating it.

(And that realization already puts us in the next loop —completely ignorant of it, of course. Fun!)

If you find yourself stuck in one of these loops (like feeling inadequate), then the way out is to surrender to the loop.

To no longer want the feeling of inadequacy to be gone, for example.

I'm not saying you'll never successfully get rid of it. But I am inviting you to accept that as a possibility.

Accepting it not as a technique to "stop the loop", but to fully welcome the loop you're in.

Treat it as something that may be there for the rest of your life. Something you've decided to find a way to love.

Let's imagine for a moment, that that's the truth of it: That the loop will always be there . That the feeling will be there forever.

Your search is finally over and you have found the answer: Your problem can not be fixed.

What would you do then?

(Keeping in mind that you could do anything you want. But not cause intentional harm for anybody, including yourself.)

If your problem was unfixable, and you were now alleviated of the burden of finding a cure, how would you make peace with being in this loop for the rest of your life?

Welcoming the loop is the only way "out".

Because when it's not lovingly welcomed, the loop will react *to* itself *through* itself.

For example: when inadequacy isn't welcomed, you'll feel inadequate about feeling so inadequate. Similarly, not welcoming anger makes you angry about being angry. Not welcoming fear makes you afraid of your anxiety.

But if instead of running away, we move towards it —if we investigate what our current loop is made of without judging what we find— we can find the common humanity inside.

Knowing that our human condition will be here for the rest of our life, we can bring love to it.

Until love becomes our new loop. A loop we can access at any point. Starting small but growing exponentially:

"I love my imperfections.

I love myself for loving them.

I love myself for loving myself for loving them."

That's the doorway.

Embracing your lack of confidence *is* your confidence.

The most confident thing you can do is be openly unconfident.

Confidence is not about being the best at something.

It's not even about being better than others.

In fact, such thoughts of superiority can stem from overcompensation for insecurity and low self-esteem.

And the desire to rank in something or compete with others sometimes stems from self-doubt and a constant need for affirmation.

It's a convincing facade. But it's built on an unstable foundation.

Real, grounded confidence is not about comparing yourself at all.

It's about knowing you have value.

Even when you're in a space where you're not the best at *anything*.

The most confident people won't brag or talk down to others.

The most confident people aren't always the loudest or most dominant in the room.

Because they don't have to prove themselves.

You don't have to prove yourself.

You are a loop made of love.

About to discover your nature.

Discovering our nature.

Personally, I believe that's the game we're all playing here:

That we all get dropped into this world at a different distance from divinity.

Finding our way home by solving the riddle that we are.

...but who am I? ;-)

CHAPTER 8
WHOSE LIFE IS IT ANYWAY?

Entire libraries have been written about lifestyle design.

But in essence, it all boils down to these 3 things:

1. Find what brings you joy and do more of it.
2. Find what robs you of joy and do less of it.
3. Invest your energy, time and money in a way that supports this both in the short and long-term.

This is a way of living that hasn't failed me so far.

And yet, there's two sides to this story.

On a scale of 1 to 10, how much are you enjoying what you're doing right now?

We all have some things we enjoy and other things we don't.

The reason why might surprise you though:

Usually when we ask ourselves *"Am I enjoying this?"*

What we mean is: *"Is this thing bringing me joy?"*

But that's not what the verb *"enjoy"* originally meant.

If you trace its roots back all the way to the middle ages, when it first popped up in old French, it meant *"to give joy to"*.

So you are not the one "receiving" joy from the activity. You are the person giving it.

The source of joy is you.

Next time you find yourself not enjoying something, try asking:

"How can I give more joy to this moment?

How can I bring more joy to what's happening here?"

And observe what changes.

—But what about lifestyle then?

Does it really matter what your life looks like when you can just lay in the gutter and learn to bring more joy to it?—

Who am I to tell you if it matters?

The question is: Does it matter to *you*?

There are happy billionaires and happy beach bums.

Just as there are miserable millionaires and people suffering such poverty it can definitely not be solved by positive thinking.

Surround yourself with the highest quality of life available to you. But enjoy and appreciate the least you can get.

This will maintain your ability to thrive and enjoy yourself in a wide variety of situations.

And you can apply it to anything:

- Art
- Food
- Ideas
- Humor
- People
- Furniture

The same meal that can feel like an abundant feast can be ruined by asking *"Is it organic at least?"*

And in those moments when you truly have nothing, let your grief contain the gratitude for every blessing you took for granted.

Let your emptiness become a canvas of possibility, not a pit of despair.

Your relationship with life is a dance between opposites.

You lead her with intentional direction towards the things that bring you joy.

You respect that she is under no obligation to follow you.

And whatever moves she makes, you appreciate her wild beauty without interfering.

You welcome her as she is, then gently invite her where you'd like to go next.

(And as odd as it may sound, she'll be doing the same with you. Simultaneously.)

Structure and flow is the delicate balance of this dance.

Lean too much towards flow and things will fall apart.

Rely too much on structure and they'll start to feel stale.

Rigid parenting can prevent self-exploration and delay adulthood.

Too much freedom can make a child so anxious it stays in a corner.

As adults, we take on the role of both our parents towards ourselves.

And the more we learn to dance with these polarities, the better we support our own continuous development.

Some periods, we'll benefit from a structured routine. To reduce the need for daily decision making. And effortlessly align our actions with our needs.

Other times, we're better off going with the flow. To remind ourselves that's all we can do (you can pretend all you want, but life's leading you way more than you are leading her).

If your routine is restricting you from doing what you want, it no longer serves you.

Remember: You're the one who chose to design it.

When you've been doing the chicken dance on repeat for too long, you might wanna switch it up a bit.

What was once a good habit can easily become a neurosis or addiction over time.

Few habits are inherently good or bad. It's the intention behind them that makes it so.

The glass of rum to escape your life is not the same as the one you drink to celebrate it.

The workout you put yourself through because you hate the way you look isn't the same as the one you do because you love keeping your body healthy.

When I struggle being consistent with something, I usually come to the same conclusion:

Deep down, I no longer want to do it.

At some point, I've started telling myself I *"should"*.

Because that structure makes me feel safe.

When something intrinsically matters to you, consistency takes care of itself.

In those cases, discipline isn't something you need to impose on yourself.

It's something that naturally happens.

Discipline means you become/are becoming *"disciple in"* the habit.

You pursue it because you want to master it.

And when you miss a day, it knocks on the door to your soul. Asking if it may come back in.

When your days seem like nothing but chaos and you're craving to balance it out with control, consider this question first:

What if your camera's stuck in zoom mode right now?

Dropping your diet for a day can seem like a huge inconsistency.

But what happens when you look at it over the course of a year?

What does your average "performance" look like when viewed on a broader time scale?

If you eat a huge tub of ice cream once a month, you're still 98.71% consistent with your daily diet on a yearly basis.

If you eat a huge tub of ice cream zero times a year, you might be 0% consistent with honoring your heart's desire.

Balance comes in different shapes and forms.

Your mornings and evenings could be each other's counterweight.

Or you might burn midnight oil all summer, then hibernate.

Some live fast and die young.

Some say temperament is the secret to old age.

A decade of laziness can light the spark to your wildest adventures.

A deep depression can compensate for years of prioritizing work over wellbeing.

Eventually balance is always found.

So when it eludes you, try zooming out.

Life isn't static. It's always moving.

This means your lifestyle isn't a static thing to "achieve" either.

The way we obsess about lifestyle shows that we misunderstand how it really works.

Life isn't separate from you.

You yourself are —quite literally— an expression of life.

So your "lifestyle" isn't as much a question of *"What are you doing with your life?"* but rather *"What is life doing with its you?"*

Life itself is the cause of all your actions, thoughts and emotions.

And it's impossible to stop that from happening.

Many wise people have used the analogy of life being a river.

And you being the captain on a boat.

In that analogy you can either steer your boat *with* the current or go *against* it.

And that's not entirely wrong.

But I don't think you're a captain. And I'm gonna take a risky guess that you aren't in a boat.

What if what you are is not a captain but a wave?

One motion in the ocean of life. Inseparable from the whole.

Carried by it in all that you do.

Here for as long as the ocean decides.

Until it lovingly swallows you back up.

And you wonder what you've been afraid of this whole time.

It would be ridiculous to ask a wave:

"What do you wanna do with your ocean?

What sort of `ocean style' will you design?"

It makes a lot more sense to ask the ocean:

"Hey ocean, what do you wanna do with this wave?

What's the shape you want it to take?"

To which the ocean would probably reply something like:

"Anything shape it wants to take. As long as it doesn't intend to cause harm."

What would happen if you designed your life around that question:

What does the ocean seem to wanna do with this wave?

(Because let's be honest, it's the ocean who decides either way).

If that idea sounds a little scary —perhaps like losing control— consider this:

In reality, there is no controller and there is nothing to be controlled.

You are not "separate from life".

You are life.

Expressing itself the way it does through you form.

Whether "you" want it or not.

You can try *real hard* to resist the flow of life.

To be an independent actor.

But that would still just be the ocean saying:

"You know what I'll do with this wave?

I'll have it convince itself it's not a part of me and make it feel heroic.

That would be a fun game!"

-Don't we have any free will at all then?-

That's a question to ask smarter people than me.

But if I had to give it a shot:

You controlling life or life controlling you are exactly the same thing.

You have free will because you *are* life.

There's no way out of it.

You can't *not* be life.

Even if you were to die, your body would become fertile soil from which lots of other life could spring.

The point of this is not to needlessly philosophize.

It's to hope some words can land into your cells and make them realize you can't do it wrong.

You can't not be yourself. You can't *"ruin life"*.

You are the ocean freely expressing itself in any way it wants to.

What that expression feels like will depend on your willingness to welcome yourself as you really are.

Anyone who has spent significant time at sea would agree that some waves and weathers are easier to welcome than others.

But to the ocean it's all the same: Just another day of eternal play.

CHAPTER 9
YOUR NATURE

—"*You're so disciplined with everything!*"—

Here's my secret;

80% of what I do are things I really, really, really want to do.

I don't need discipline to be consistent with them.

After all, I'm just doing what I want.

The other 20%?

I'm so inconsistent with them, that I look like a toddler.

The key to consistency isn't choosing a frequency and forcing yourself to stick with it.

It's finding a rhythm that's sustainable for you, slowly increasing your capacity to identify the "right" actions in the "right" moment, and learning to trust those intuitions even when they seem irrational.

When your life is an authentic expression of who you are, you don't have to force yourself to create it.

Let's take this little book as an example:

I've been wanting to write it for months.

I could've been telling myself:

"*Why didn't you finish it yet???*

Get consistent, work on it for 90 minutes every day!"

And a previous version of myself would've listened to that voice, never skipping a single session.

But that would be like yelling at a plant *"Why haven't you grown yet? Grow faster!!"*.

(Editor's note: This is not just a metaphor. Yelling at a plant measurably leads to the plant producing more ethylene, a stress hormone. Which is good in small amounts but can adversely affect its growth and development when produced in excess. Also: It's me, Pep. I'm the editor. Just thought it sounded cool to call this an editor's note.)

The proper way to nurture a plant's growth is to keep a patient eye on it. Give it water, sunlight or shade when it needs them. And trust the mystery that makes it grow.

Similarly, you can learn to listen to the rhythm of your own body and mind.

Tend to them when they have needs.

Discipline and consistency will naturally arise when they're needed.

So will breaks and diversions.

That's exactly what happened with this book:

The idea was there. I mostly ignored it.

But whenever it begged for attention or words fell into my head, I wrote them down.

This book spent most of the winter being a seed.

By spring it was a bunch of loose phrases which I couldn't connect to each other.

Now (mid-summer), it has grown to its full size over the course of a few hours.

It did "only" take a few months. But most of them were spent trusting it would happen someday.

And very few of them were spent writing.

Even less telling myself to write more.

Someone once told me *"Your natural pace is the right pace"*.

And I'd add to that: *"Your natural pace will happen anyway"*.

You can go real fast now and life will teach you to slow down later.

Or you can go at a sustainable pace the whole time.

Both are natural and perfect in their own way.

Just like we learned in the last chapter: balance is always achieved.

It all depends on how broad a timeframe you're looking at.

I know plenty of people who are into health, spirituality or sociology and obsess about what's natural versus what isn't.

The presumption being that "natural" is always good and "unnatural" is always bad.

Yet ingesting a single seed of the castor oil plant can kill you.

While synthetically produced penicillin has saved millions of lives.

Perhaps a better question than *"is this natural?"*, would be:

"All things considered, what is the impact this makes?"

Cause let me tell you a little secret:

"Unnatural" is just a word.

And like many words, it's a layer of illusion that covers up reality.

I challenge you to do something unnatural right now.

You can't.

Because you *are* nature.

Everything you do will always be natural.

When we see a bird gather twigs to build a nest, we sigh: *"Aah... nature is beautiful!"*

But when we see humans build a crane and use it to build skyscrapers, we say: *"Oh, that's not natural!"*

What's *that* all about?

When scientists isolate chemicals in a lab and combine them to form novel compounds, we call the resulting substance unnatural.

But where did the raw materials come from, if not nature?

And who combined them, if not nature acting through the form of human beings?

Everything that exists in the physical world is by definition a part of nature.

To view ourselves as separate from that is just dissociation from our own body.

It's culturally normalized to be in awe of a sunrise, a beautiful beach or a starry night sky.

But the endless beauty of nature can also be found in a fellow human's eyes, the invention of AI or the experience of your body keeping itself alive.

Who makes your heart beat?

Who makes your lungs breathe?

Who gives you your greatest ideas?

Who's the "it" when it rains?

Every thing around us, inside us, and even imagined by us can be an awesome thing to behold.

All it takes is that we allow ourselves to stop dissociating and be in awe of their nature again.

CHAPTER 10
YOUR REAL PRIORITIES

"No matter what you tell the world or tell yourself, your actions reveal your real values.

Your actions show you what you actually want.

There are two smart reactions to this:

Stop lying to yourself, and admit your real priorities.

Start doing what you say you want to do, and see if it's really true."

— Derek Sivers

Priorities aren't chosen.

They already live inside your heart.

All you have to do is listen for them.

If you try to override them with what you think your priorities *"should"* be, one of the following things will happen:

A. You'll end up prioritizing what you *really* want anyway and feel guilty about it.

B. You'll end up doing what you think you *"should"* do and feel sad about not doing what you want.

Both of these experiences are forms of self-torture by illusion.

But when they happen, they do so for a reason: To guide you towards the truth of what matters most to you.

The truth is, in both cases, you actually *are* following your real priorities.

When you end up doing what you *"should"* do and not following *"your heart's longing"*, in reality, you are still following the latter.

For example:

Someone may think what they want most is to travel the world. But instead they study to become a lawyer. Because that's what their parents want for them.

It would be common to say of such a person that they're not following their heart.

But they *are.*

Inside their heart is a longing for the love of their parents.

And that longing is more important to them than traveling the world.

Just like it's impossible to do something unnatural, it's impossible to not follow your real priorities.

You are always doing what is most important to you at this moment.

Even if it doesn't make sense on a logical level.

You can eat a cheeseburger and lament *"...but my diet was so important to me!"*

And you'd be right.

But the pleasure and comfort of the cheeseburger were also important to you.

And in that moment, they were your priority.

Trust the process.

It's hard when you know there are things you want to do and you're not doing them because something seems to be *"stopping you"*:

- People pleasing
- Addiction
- Codepency
- Fear of failure

The list can go on.

But those things —even if unpleasant— are happening because they serve a need that's important to you.

I've spent decades disconnected from myself, my body and my feelings.

But in a sense you could say I never lost connection at all.

My deepest desire in that period *was* to disconnect.

Because I wanted to not feel overwhelmed by it all.

Disconnecting from myself was an act of self-connection and honored my priorities.

A lot of what's deemed dysfunctional could be seen as *"functional in an unpopular or unpleasant way"*.

And yes, these "dysfunctions" do make things harder for us.

When I suffered from insomnia, sleep was often an impossibility. But it did protect me from spending too much time with my subconscious mind. Which was where the demons lived.

Once I was fit to face the demons, I found my way to deep and restful sleep.

Sometimes such a change occurs out of nowhere. Sometimes, we need to hit rock bottom first.

That doesn't mean all your "dysfunctional" patterns are your choice. Trauma is real.

It doesn't mean your fears are always appropriate to the moment either. Or that staying in an unhealthy dynamic is good for you.

What it means is that all three of those things are serving your real priorities, until they are not

And when they no longer do, "healing" will happen at its natural pace.

Whether it involves external care and medicine or not.

When the love of another becomes less important than the love of the self, codependency dissolves.

When the desire for peace becomes stronger than the desire for safety, hypervigilance transforms into spaceholding.

And when personal freedom takes precedence over belonging, you'll find yourself dancing in ways that previously would have embarrassed you.

In those moments, what seemed to be opposing concerns often merge back into one.

You discover that your sense of belonging runs much deeper when you feel free within a group.

That your inner peace makes you feel safer than anxiety ever did.

And that love is love, even if it didn't come from the person you used to crave it from, or in the exact form you craved it.

When it comes to priorities or personal growth, you can't do it wrong.

You're always doing it *just right* for where you are right now in your journey.

You might sit down with pen and paper and sort out your priorities through a process of reason.

But why did you end up doing so? Because gaining clarity was your real first priority.

On the other hand, you might write it all out and then proceed to engage in actions which don't reflect what was written on the list at all.

That's because those actions were your true priorities.

And maybe the whole reason for writing the list was to observe this discrepancy and learn something about yourself.

Who's to say?

Life's mostly a mystery.

But my point is: You got this.

Either way, you did exactly what you wanted to do.

And you will continue to do so.

Embrace this fact and you'll be free.

CHAPTER 11
DESTINATION: DEATH

Failure is nothing but a label.

It exists as long as the label is used.

In reality, it's impossible to fail.

You either die, succeed or decide to quit.

Neither of those is a failure.

Quitting gets a bad rep.

When someone quits, the story our culture makes about it is they *"gave up"* or *"broke a commitment"*.

But the truth is, if you quit, then there was no commitment to begin with.

Commitment is when you agree to stick with something. No matter how you feel about it. No matter what happens.

Commitment is saying *"from now on, I restrict myself of the freedom to opt out of this"*.

Anything less than that isn't a commitment. It's an engagement.

Which is totally okay.

You don't owe anyone a commitment.

You are simply committed to what you are committed to.

If you quit, you didn't *"break"* a commitment.

You didn't *"give up"* or *"fail"*.

You succeeded at choosing to honor your real priorities.

It's better to quit because you *want to* than to go on because you don't want to look like a failure. (Of course, with the caveat that if *"not looking like a failure"* is your reason for not quitting, it is probably just a priority of yours. Which is to be respected.)

Once again, we arrive at the same conclusion:

It is not possible to fail.

You are always succeeding. Just not always at the things you believe you are.

Now you might think: *"I sure have racked up some very tangible failures in my life."*

If that's the case, I can relate.

I used to spend all my rides home obsessively analyzing every *"wrong"* word I had spoken. Knowing exactly what I *"should have said"*. But knowing it only a few hours after already effing things up royally.

Thoughts like that can be quite unpleasant (or pleasantly educational, if you let them).

But don't let hindsight fool you into thinking you could've done things differently.

The reason you have hindsight in the first place is that you did things the way you did them.

If you ever tell yourself: *"I should have done that differently"*, you need to hear this:

You couldn't have done it differently...

If what you did felt like the right thing at the time, why would you have done something else?

And if you knew it was the "wrong" thing, that means you didn't have the desire or capacity to choose otherwise at that moment.

Either way, it ended up being the thing you did.

That couldn't be changed retrospectively, nor could it have been changed in the moment.

Or else, it wouldn't have been that same moment anymore.

If reading that, you find yourself saying *"Okay, I couldn't have. But I still should have."*

There is no need to be so hard on yourself (unless you want to).

It may seem like what you *"should"* have done would've led to a better outcome. But if you've ever seen the movie "The Butterfly Effect", you know that's not how life works.

Ask yourself this:

What can I do differently next time?

And realize how great it is that you have the chance to ask that.

Whatever you wish you would've done differently is the very thing that gave you this knowledge.

Words like "failure" and "success" suggest that somewhere in life, we will arrive at a static point. At a destination of some kind.

"Now I'm here."

"Now that I've achieved this, I've finally arrived."

But life, being the ocean that it is, doesn't care much about your arrival. It keeps moving and making waves.

Can you achieve the end of hunger?

No. But it can disappear for a while, until the next hunger wave comes.

Can you achieve the end of suffering?

Maybe.

But as long as you're alive, there's no guarantee that you will never suffer again.

Can you achieve tremendous wealth?

Not permanently.

But you can experience it.

Scrooge McDuck has lots of money.

But he still can't experience wealth. Because he tries to hoard it and hold on to it.

In trying to make his wealth a static achievement, he gets to experience none of its riches.

MC Hammer and Mike Tyson on the other hand, both made millions, spent them lavishly, then went bankrupt.

They *"achieved"* more wealth than most of us.

Then they *"achieved"* more debt than a college student collecting copious degrees.

In doing so, are they successes or failures?

Neither.

They surfed the waves of life.

There is nothing to achieve, to succeed or to fail at.

Life keeps moving and there's always the next thing happening.

Every moment is a brand new miracle. In which you get to make choices, enjoy the fruits and lessons of your previous ones, and are subjected to the impact of everyone else's. Which is completely out of your control.

A wave may look like it's moving on its own, but without the rest of the ocean, it wouldn't exist.

Neither would you, without the rest of the world.

And without all the other waves existing, none of us could move.

Nothing can move without something else to move in relationship *to*.

Because all motion is, is a change in position relative to something else.

So the only way to reach any real destination in life.

Is to stop existing as separate from everything else.

There may be no end point in life where you've finally "achieved" it all.

But there definitely *is* a tipping point.

When all the foundations are in place.

When the toughest part of the journey is behind you.

And "your" life has become a balanced ecosystem which deeply nourishes you every day.

After your tipping point, your wave moves more easily.

Because it derives more energy from its own motion than it loses to any external or internal resistance.

In this phase, it would take more effort to go back where you came from than to keep gaining in size and beauty.

My deepest wish is for you to reach that point.

I've been there for quite a while now, enjoying the beautiful scenery and letting my wave unfold.

But make no mistake, I'm only 33. Who am I to tell you about life and its tipping points?

There's still plenty of peaks I could reach.

And when I've reached the highest one this wave has in store for itself, then what?

Eventually, all waves have to come back down.

All the way back into the ocean, until there's nothing left of us.

To die and be welcomed back into the whole. That's our destination.

At least, as far as we can tell. Who knows what happens after!

But let that neither scare us, nor make us want to hasten towards it.

What a waste of a wave it would be, for you not to witness your fullest form.

Because what are the odds of you existing?

And each day your shape's a little different.

So every new chance you get to catch a glimpse of your own existence is a cause for reverence and a celebration.

CHAPTER 12
INFINITE LIMITING BELIEFS

There is no such thing as a non-limiting belief, except for the one that includes all the others.

Most beliefs are limiting because they say *"reality is this way, not that way"*.

If you believe you are worthless, you can't feel worthy.

And if you believe you're worthy, you won't be able to feel worthless anymore.

Beliefs can empower or disempower. They can be accurate or inaccurate. But unless they contain their opposites, they are by definition limiting.

Limiting beliefs are commonly seen as obstacles to be overcome.

But it's not necessary to disprove every limiting belief you hold.

All you need is a context that contains the possibility of playing with their opposites.

And that context is already here, waiting for you to step into it again.

I invite you to remember it was you who chose your beliefs.

Even if you can't recall why you chose them.

Even if they were hand-me-downs from parents, teachers or other authority figures, you were the one who took them on.

(Which doesn't make you "to blame" for them. But that's something we'll get to in a later chapter).

You could say that beliefs are the mental clothing we wear.

Except each belief you wear is also automatically worn by the world you walk in.

So while you're dressing up your mind, you're simultaneously dressing up your reality.

And in keeping with this metaphor of clothing:

The more clothes you put on something, the more of its parts become hidden and invisible.

If a person's wearing twenty pairs of pants, you probably won't witness their inner thighs any time soon.

So it is with life itself, the nature of humanity and the nature of reality: The more beliefs you cover them with, the less of them you'll be able to perceive.

And while being unclothed might not be ideal in every situation: Do you really need to believe something about everything?

You might wanna keep a number of foundational beliefs. Those which feel necessary to act as a functional human in this world.

You might even feign some extra ones to keep conversations familiar for friends and family.

But if you want to truly know yourself, others and the world you inhabit, then it's best to relate to your beliefs as loose clothing you picked out for the season.

They may feel comfortable to be in.

But the real fun begins once you take them off.

CHAPTER 13
YOU HAVE ALREADY DECIDED

As you walk through life, aware that what seemed like problems are actually choices to be made, you might run into some which make you wonder: *"What's the right choice here?"*

So why don't we take a moment to investigate exactly how choices are made?

Choices are made by our system —consciously or unconsciously— evaluating a hierarchy of values and attempting to ensure the outcome aligns with what matters most to us.

This means all our decisions reflect our real priorities.

Whether they were determined by consciously weighing all the options or by our instincts recognizing what we care about and jumping in before a thought even occurred.

Your choices are yet another example of you always doing what you want.

There may have been times when you made a choice which seemed like the opposite of what you wanted. But in those cases, there was a factor at play which mattered more to you.

Whether it was safety, belonging, relief from pressure or something entirely different: unconsciously, the values were weighed and the decision was aligned with them.

Just because we think something is important to us, doesn't mean it actually *is*.

Our real values are revealed in our actions, not our words.

We might tell ourselves we have a strong value for something because we believe it's the *"right"* or the *"respectable"* value to have.

But since behavior is the real indicator, all that means is that we value seeing ourselves as a good person.

For this same reason, we sometimes ascribe our decisions to different values than the ones that drove them.

We like to be the hero in our story. So when we value something we judge others for, that value will disguise itself as a socially acceptable virtue.

The real value will operate in the shadows and the "virtue" will be used as an excuse for our antisocial behavior (or to cover up a part of our personality which we are in denial of).

For example:

Many people say they value honesty And that that's the virtue that causes them to constantly criticize others.

They'll say *"I'm not a jerk, I'm just honest. I tell it straight to people's faces."*

Yet, when it comes to telling their spouse that they cheated, suddenly that honesty isn't the main value anymore.

Similarly, there are groups who believe they value equality or liberty. But when you look at their actions, they actually embody values like power, revenge and punishment.

On the opposite spectrum, there are groups who say they value tradition but actually value control, repression and exclusion.

All of this is not to say it's wrong to have values which aren't considered virtuous in your culture.

But to caution you not to take your thoughts too seriously.

You are what you are and you do what you do.

Life be livin'.

Sometimes the question on your mind will not be *"What do I want?"* but *"What's the best choice I could make here?"*

That question by itself is impossible to answer. Because as we've seen, *"best"* needs a context to be defined.

And the implicit context will simply be what you value most.

For one person this might mean: *"What's the most loving choice?"*

For another *"What's the choice that gives me the most resources in return?"*

For myself, I believe the best choices to be the ones that —when possible— honor everyone involved at the same time.

And as much as I attempt to do so, I'll often still default to choices that mostly honor myself

Let's be honest:

If there is a best choice, but you feel like you want the other one more...which choice are you going to take?

If the answer was *"the best one, of course!"*

Then the truth is: You didn't want to make the other choice more than you wanted to make the best choice ;-)

Whatever value you used as context to define *"best"* mattered more to you than what you initially thought you wanted.

"You've been looking for the best person, place, or career.
But seeking the best is the problem.
No choice is inherently the best.
What makes something the best choice?
You. You make it the best through your commitment to it.
Your dedication and actions make any choice great."

— Derek Sivers

Would you have sex with someone you're disgusted by in exchange for a hundred bucks?

How about a million?

Or a billion?

For how much money would you lie to your partner, break your diet or do something shameful in public?

The amount at which you said yes is the point where you value those things less than money.

The amount where you still said no is the point where you valued them more.

This is how values really work.

They reveal themselves when challenged by real-world choices.

Real-world, meaning "not hypothetical".

Just like you play poker differently when real money is at stake, your answers to this thought-exercise could be very different from the decisions you'd make in the moment.

In fact, at any moment, your values might shift based on your needs and desires.

So why worry about them?

Whether you write them down or not.

You will be as you are anyway.

—*"Hold on a minute…*

Aren't there many examples of people acting out of alignment with their values?

Isn't it possible that sometimes we make choices which don't serve our own interests?"—

Yes it is.

Sometimes when we look at our own behavior through a microscopic lens, it seems like our actions are out of alignment.

But when we zoom out a little, we see that acting out of alignment is exactly how one stays in alignment.

If you never do something that makes you feel misaligned, you will never know where your alignment begins and ends.

Balance is achieved by leaning in and out of stability in every possible direction and adjusting your position in accordance.

Nothing in this universe is static.

Stillness is a continuous movement of adjusting and readjusting.

The more still something seems, the faster and the more subtle the movement.

The more aligned someone seems, the higher their frequency of misalignment and re-alignment.

But truly *"misalignment"* is a misnomer, as these momentary *"misaligned"* choices are the exact process keeping you aligned.

If you lived an entire life from birth till death without ever making a choice that felt wrong, how would you know at the end that the choices you made were right?

Without experiencing wrong, right would be a meaningless concept to you.

The way to spice a dish *just right* is achieved through the repeated act of tasting it and concluding it's not right yet.

That is the process. That is the balance happening.

The master chef has underspiced and overseasoned so many times, their intuition is now refined to a point where they're perfectly attuned to their cookery.

But that attunement is directly tied to all the dishes that ended up in the trash.

One can't exist without the other.

It took years of drinking daily for me to realize the misalignment underneath.

And an equal amount spent strictly sober to see that wasn't what I wanted either.

Those weren't years of bad decisions. They were years of alignment happening in real time.

And that's a process which never stops.

So don't be too quick to judge your decisions by their immediate results.

Open your senses to what their data is telling you.

Allow yourself to really live for a few decades.

And soon enough, you'll go from "a walking collection of mistakes" to walking life's tightrope with grace.

How often do you ask your pinky toe if it agrees with your decisions?

If you're like most people, you'd probably rather make them by thinking.

But you may have noticed that you sometimes get stuck in loops or regret the decisions.

Because when you made them, you used only a limited part of your intelligence.

And I'm not talking about that 10% of your brain theory, that's a myth.

What I mean is, your body inherited forms of intelligence far older and more developed than your brains.

They have fine-tuned their alignment through millions of years of evolution and life experience. From the earth's first microbe, all the way down to your mom.

When you learn to listen to their signals, it can speed up your alignment process tremendously.

Next time you are faced with a conscious decision, I invite you to try this:

1. Check with your brain as usual
2. Check with your heart. How does each option feel emotionally? Can you feel your heart coming alive? Or does it contract at the thought of it?
3. What about your gut, what do your instincts say? Is your gut calm, or does it resist one of the outcomes?
4. What about your genitals, are they into this? Or is it a floppy taco down there?

Simple rule: if any of them feel like a "no," the option is a no-go.

Stick with it.

It's either a whole-body yes, or nothing at all.

Compare it to summoning a council of wise people (who are all you) to debate the decision.

And they can only move forward once a unanimous agreement has been reached.

If you use only one type of intelligence, people can convince you with rational arguments, emotionally manipulate you or seduce your taco into making the wrong decision.

But if you listen to your body, including your mind, you'll sense when something's off

The more you do this, the more everything in your life starts to align with who you are.

Sometimes the signal may not be super clear to you and you'll need to listen a little longer.

The classic advice to "sleep on it" isn't a coincidence:

Just as muddy water becomes clear when left undisturbed, the mind can find clarity when it's calm and free from agitation.

And if a situation's truly urgent (rather than just framed as urgent), the body will propel you into action without needing to think it through.

Having trouble deciding between two or more options?

Throw a coin or dice in the air and let it decide for you.

Observe your body as the object is spinning in front of you.

Usually one of three things will happen:

A). While in the air, you'll find yourself wishing for it to land on a specific option.

B). As the object is about to land on a certain side, you'll feel part of your body contract, trying to control the outcome.

C). It'll land and you'll feel excited or disappointed by the result.

All these options reveal how you truly feel about this.

When a choice is presented to you as a linear "A vs B" question, remind yourself that is not how life operates.

Every letter of the alphabet is at your disposal.

And if you don't like them, there's always the option of inventing some new ones.

Sometimes the question *"A or B?"* can be answered with *"both, and here's how I'll do it!"*.

Other times, it can be answered with *"D"*.

The way a question is framed can make our mind narrow down the options.

After all, it would be quite overwhelming to consider life's infinite possibilities every time we're faced with a choice.

But when a choice makes you feel stuck, remember that the unmentioned options do exist.

Allow yourself to feel into the open field that reality really is. And explore nonlinear solutions.

After writing this, I'm wondering:

"Do I delete this page from the book?

Or do I find a proper example to clarify what it means?"

I decided to take option U (the 21st letter of the alphabet).

That's right:

You get to decide what it means for you.

Who am I to tell you what conclusions to draw from a book you chose to read?

People often say one of the superior things about humans compared to other animals is that our prefrontal cortex gives us the logic and reason to override our impulses.

But what is creating the impulse to use logic and reason in one moment, and throw it out the window in another?

Rationality is a powerful tool for investigation, simulation and forecasting scenarios.

But when it comes to decision making, it's mostly used to create justifications or cover-ups for the decisions already made. Not to actually drive our behavior.

Even when logic was used as the process for making the decision, it did so because the forces that govern you deemed it to be the appropriate tool.

Had a knee-jerk response been more appropriate, that's what would've happened instead.

Which brings us to the topic of "excuses"...

CHAPTER 14
ALL YOUR EXCUSES ARE EXCUSED

Excuses live a lonely life.

They spend their time trying to protect our fragile egos.

And what do they get in return?

Nothing but misunderstanding.

We view them as barriers detrimental to our personal growth and success.

Barriers to be crushed and avoided at all costs.

But that narrative fails to find the love within them.

Yes, excuses *are* barriers.

But they're not barriers to success.

They're barriers to self-abandonment.

They jump in front and take the bullet when we don't feel capable of standing our own ground and owning what we want.

Every excuse is in essence a justification.

When someone's *"dog ate their homework"*, the culturally appropriate response is:

"That's a dogshit excuse. Now go and do your homework like everyone else."

But to get to the heart of the matter, you'd have to ask:

"What's the real reason you didn't bring your homework?"

There are many possible answers to that question.

- *"I don't feel confident in my knowledge of this topic. And I'm terrified of bad grades."*
- *"My parents were fighting all night and I felt overwhelmed. The last thing I wanted to do was this homework."*
- Or even: *"I was watching cartoons. And frankly sir, I found them way more interesting than trigonometry."*

As you may have noticed.

Each of these answers can be distilled into the by now familiar:

"I didn't want to."

So yes, we can recognize that our excuses are BS.

But the fact that an excuse is inauthentic, doesn't mean the behavior it justifies is inauthentic.

If you don't want to do something and you have a bunch of excuses protecting you from doing so, then the real question is: Unless you're a masochist, why make yourself do it?

Plenty of people are confused about this idea.

They'll say: *"I do want it. It's my excuses that are getting in the way.."*

But that's just another excuse.

Wanting the idea of something is very different from wanting the thing.

Many people want the idea of a body perfectly shaped to the present beauty standards. Yet few people want the reality it entails.

Whether it's the work required to maintain it, the unwanted attention, or the fact that being hugged and armored by some extra weight can feel good too.

None of those are excuses.

It's the difference between something being a fun scenario to fantasize about and a thing you actually want.

Or let's take public speaking as an example:

It's one of the most common fears among humans. So naturally, a lot of humans have thoughts telling them not to do it.

Some of those people will do it anyway. Others won't.

Is it that the group who didn't do it failed to conquer their excuses?

No. It's that the group who did it wanted to do it.

They still had doubtful thoughts, but the thoughts didn't stop them.

The thoughts were smaller than the desire to do it.

Which doesn't make it an act of *"conquering"* your excuses.

But an act of going for what you want, regardless of potential reasons not to.

Because what you want doesn't live in your thoughts. It lives in your being.

And try as they may, thoughts can't stop you from doing what you really want to do.

When you say *"I shouldn't drink a massive milkshake with every meal. Because it'll make me fat!"*, no one's going to tell you *"That's an excuse! Get over yourself!"*

And if someone else would say the exact same thing, then proceed to drink the milkshakes anyway, no one would celebrate them for heroically conquering those excuses.

Why not?

In both cases, you'd simply have done what you wanted.

Whether your thoughts agreed with that or not.

One person didn't want the milkshake. The other person did.

Professional excuse-busters (and salespeople) will say stuff like *"You don't need a permission slip from your significant other to start a business (or buy what I'm selling)!"* or *"It's not that you don't have enough time, it's that you manage it poorly."*

But the truth is:

Some people care how their actions impact their spouse's stress levels more than they care about joining your Multi-Level Marketing scam. So their choices will align with that.

And the most perfectly planned schedule won't prevent you from ignoring it and spending time on what you really want to do deep down.

Piling some time management techniques on top of that only results in the frustration with not living up to your plan and looking for more tools to make yourself.

Why?

Because the plan wasn't what you wanted.

And the excuses or distractions tried to help you when you didn't have the courage to own that.

Saying no to working on a project because you want to play video games is no different from saying no to a milkshake because you love your waistline.

Own it, and it'll no longer own you.

When you tell a life coach why you're not *"doing the thing"* right now, they'll:

- Call it an excuse (often true).
- Try to shift your beliefs about it.
- Make you feel more empowered.

Generally, they'll focus on removing the *"blockage"* between you and the thing.

But what most people fail to notice is this:

In the majority of cases, there is no blockage.

You simply don't wanna do the thing.

But you *do* wanna see yourself as the kind of person who *would* do the thing.

The excuses aren't holding you back.

They're helping you hold up this false sense of self.

What if you let go of all ideas about who you think you *should* be and instead pay close attention to who you *are*?

What if you learned to fully trust what you *actually* want, rather than what you *want* to want?

Some of it might seem nonsensical. Or unimpressive. But nothing could be further from the truth.

To wholeheartedly embrace yourself and act in alignment with that —to me— is the most impressive and "sensical" thing you can do.

Trust yourself.

You got this.

CHAPTER 15
MILKSHAKES, MARSHMALLOWS & MILLIONAIRES

What's the difference between choosing not to have milkshakes and choosing not to be a millionaire?

What's the difference that —according to the self-help community— makes the latter a bunch of excuses and the former a bunch of common sense?

It's the idea that smart choices require sacrificing short-term fun for long-term fulfillment.

The marshmallow test is a famous experiment where children were given a choice between eating one marshmallow right away or waiting a while to get two.

This experiment was designed to study self-control and delayed gratification.

And it's commonly interpreted in a way that kids who chose *"one marshmallow now rather than two later"* showed poor self-control and suboptimal decision making.

In other words, they *"lost the test"*.

While for some kids this may have been the case, viewing the experiment exclusively through the lens of self-control leaves out plenty of possible explanations:

What if you only wanted one marshmallow, but not two?

What if your self-control was applied to the portion of marshmallows rather than the timing?

What if you valued having it more now than having it double?

That would mean instant gratification was the optimal choice.

Furthermore (a word I had to use at least once to appear intelligent as a writer), the future isn't set in stone.

What if you *"win"* the marshmallow test by delaying your gratification, but the future version of you no longer wants *any* marshmallows?

What if the experiment was a cruel set-up and the future marshmallows never came?

Imagine for a second it was 2006 and you owned a high amount of financial assets, particularly properties and related securities.

Everybody around you would say: *"You're wise to hold on to this! They will appreciate in value, it's an investment in your future"*

But when you checked in with your gut, your heart and your spicy taco, they all said:

"Fudge it all! Let's sell everything and spend the money drinking margaritas on a beach for a few decades. While we pay some scientists with the leftovers to attempt to solve world-hunger!"

That would've resulted in a better outcome than holding on to the assets, since an "unpredicted" financial crash was right around the corner.

There's no denying that investing or saving are wise strategies compared to blindly spending.

But whether they are the right choice for you, depends on whether you decide they are.

You can take care of "future you" all you want, but you don't know what future you will find important. Or if that person will even exist in the first place.

So only do it if it matters to "present you".

You can't know if the future you're sacrificing your present for is the one you'll still want at that age —or will have the health to enjoy.

You might save it all up for retirement, then die the day before.

And of course, the reverse is also true: You might grow up to be 115 years old and be unprepared for that despite having planned for retirement.

—*"So now what? Should I sacrifice my present day fun for future fulfillment or not?"*—

You know the answer by now:

Do anything you want to do, without intentionally harming anyone.

True happiness isn't focused on today versus tomorrow.

It forgives the past, treasures the present and delights in the mystery of the future.

Three perspectives which collide together to form one endless experience of the ever-changing now.

The only reason you are able to anticipate future events is that you live in the here and now, accessing the wisdom of the perceived past.

None of it exists in separation.

All of it exists in the experience you are having right now.

That means if you align your actions with what your present-day self wants, those concerns will already include the future and the past too.

Sometimes you'll want to feel a past emotion which wasn't processed yet.

Sometimes you'll fear a harsh winter coming on and want to stock up on resources.

Other times, there's only the play of the moment.

We can debate about the right mix of pleasure and sacrifice all day long, but that's not where the answers are found:

Seek your Self. Follow it into full alignment. And the balancing act will take care of your future, past and present.

Left to our own devices and absent of severe mental disorders, we all end up making a combination of future-minded and present-minded decisions.

Because that's what our survival mechanisms were designed to do.

Of course, there is variance.

Some people live fast and die young.

And when they do die young, we have to conclude they were right in choosing that mindset.

They managed to compensate for their short lifespan by indulging in it much more intensely.

Others sacrifice most of their youth for a pleasant old day. And if they reach it, they'll be proven right too.

Neither outcomes are guaranteed to happen.

Just as you could end up dying before you reap the rewards of your sacrifice, you could end up living in the fast lane and grow as old as Keith Richards.

So in the end, the best choice will have been the one you made.

As you may recall, hindsight only comes after the fact.

So you couldn't have made a different one either way.

When it comes to having the marshmallow now or having two of them later, most of us organically find balance in the middle at some point.

Our decision-making intuitions develop at different rates and to various degrees.

But the accumulated life experience eventually either attunes our abilities to the level of a skilled chef's tasting or continues the balancing process for us.

Let's say you fail to save up for a rainy day.

And when it comes, you end up stuck without food.

It'll teach you one of two things:

    A). *"I can get by with much less than I thought."*

or

    B). *"This is terrible and I will not let it happen again."*

Lessons learned are lessons learned, and your behavior will adjust accordingly.

You don't need to remind yourself.

And if you do need to, you'll either remember to do so, or you'll receive the lesson again.

Whatever happens, you will be you-ing.

CHAPTER 16
ADMIT IT, YOU CAN'T RESIST

You don't have to "break through resistance" to achieve your goals.

Fighting the resistance inside you only adds more resistance to the resistance already there.

Quick math!

Resistance + resistance = Double resistance

Instead, try welcoming and accepting the resistance.

This gently shifts your attitude towards a non-resistant one.

(The catch of course —again— is that this doesn't work if you do it with the intent of getting rid of the resistance).

In the end, resistance is nothing but another excuse.

Deflecting responsibility of your inner choice to an external thing of which the existence can't be proven or disproven.

Like saying the ghost of Genghis Khan is stopping you from reaching your goals.

When the truth is:

You're just moving at your natural pace, in accordance with your real priorities.

It's like jumping off a cliff into the water:

Some people experience resistance. It takes them longer to jump.

But that doesn't make them worse jumpers than those who jumped right away.

Other people feel so much resistance it terrifies them and they don't wanna jump at all.

Did those people fail at jumping?

Did they fail to conquer their resistance?

No, they acted in authentic alignment.

They didn't want to jump more than they wanted *not* to jump.

—*"But what if this was a person looking to overcome their fears?*

Wouldn't not jumping be a failure to do so?"—

No. Unless we look at it on a super narrow time scale.

They did want to face their fears. But in this moment, the desire not to risk jumping was more meaningful and important to them.

And in reality, this encounter definitely did play its part in the process of facing those fears.

It's okay to want things to stay the same a bit longer until you don't anymore.

All decisions eventually generate experiences that lead to alignment in the long run.

There are no invisible forces stopping you which you must fight to resist.

You *are* the invisible force.
And you're irresistible.

CHAPTER 17
FLAVORS OF LOVE

Just like you don't need to fight resistance to follow your dreams, you don't need to fight your fears either.

The idea that fear is bad is one of the most persistent myths of the self-help generations.

And I say that as someone who used to suffer from a chronic anxiety disorder.

Many a new-age philosopher has said *"fear is the opposite of love"*, but as we'll soon find out, that couldn't be further from the truth.

Very few things are the opposite of love. It's just not always that obvious where the love *is*. Because it likes to play hide and seek.

—*"...but what about the virtue of courage then?*

If we want to have a good life, shouldn't we practice courage by facing our fears?"—

Not necessarily.

You *"shouldn't"* do *anything.*

Unless tied to a specific condition —as in *"if you want to be warm, you should bring a sweater today"*— the word *"should"* is nothing but another illusion.

Remember, there is nothing that you *have* to do.

And to tell yourself so only creates suffering.

Because you'll do what you want either way, whether you think you *"should"* or *"shouldn't"*.

The only thing that will change depending on those thoughts is feeling naughty or nice for doing so.

There's no point in doing things that scare you just to practice courage (unless of course, that in itself is the experience you're craving right now).

Walking on hot coals won't make you more courageous. Neither would jumping off a high building or fighting an opponent twice your size.

All you'd be doing is practicing ignorance towards a relevant fear.

Driving without seatbelts is not seen as courageous. So why would stepping into a fire be any different?

We glorify the idea of becoming *"fearless"*.

But the irony is that wanting to be fearless stems from a profound fear of the power of fear itself.

A power fear has so that it can protect you.

If what fear is protecting you from is something you *want* to be protected from, the fear will always win over any attempted courage.

If it's something that feels scary to do but you *do* want to experience it right now, the fear will morph into excitement and you'll do the thing whether you feel courageous or not.

Courage is only needed when the situation calls for an action that is dangerous, but the outcome of it is so important to you that you don't want fear to stop you from taking it.

Courage —a virtuous energy indeed— will appear when it is needed more than fear.

When the pull of your future career matters more to you than avoiding the uncertainty of the transition, courage will be there.

When the possibility of starting the first conversation with your future spouse is more meaningful than the desire not to make a fool of yourself, courage will be there.

When standing up for your values or beliefs in front of a large group of people is a lesser pain to you than the silent suffering of not doing so, courage will be there.

Fear will be there too (because courage can't exist unless there's fear).

And both feelings will be exactly what you need.

People don't have to practice courage to save a child from drowning, they simply jump in the water.

Fear is what heightens their awareness of the situation. Courage is what makes them jump despite the risks.

Once in the water, that same fear can keep them alert of additional dangers, while the courage hopefully helps them move back to safety.

Both energies go hand in hand:

Fear without courage would make you scared of jumping in.

Courage without fear would lead to recklessness, which might result in two people drowning rather than one.

It's often said that we shouldn't trust our emotions.

But if emotions were useless, why would we have evolved to be so impacted by them?

We all pretend to be rational beings, but as any person working in advertising or behavioral psychology knows: Humans are mostly driven by emotions and then use their thoughts to rationalize the behavior that was already decided upon. Not the other way around.

In other words: We do what we want, then we convince ourselves we had a good reason to do so.

That doesn't mean rational decisions can never be made, but emotions are the more powerful drivers behind your behavior.

And even those who live a very rational life usually have strong emotional reasons for living it that way (like being afraid of the unpredictability of emotionally driven behavior).

We tend to categorize emotions as "bad" or "good".

- Sadness
- Shame
- Anger
- Fear

These are seen as "bad" emotions. If you feel them, something's "wrong".

And you're expected to take action towards not feeling them anymore.

- Excitement
- Pride
- Love
- Joy

These all supposedly fall in the "good" category. If you're not feeling them, figure out why. And "get your act together".

We learn these ideas at such a young age that they're deeply ingrained in our psyche.

But this binary view of feelings isn't always accurate.

For example, fear can save your life by triggering fight-or-flight responses.

Fear is what makes you instinctively jump aside instead of getting hit by a car. Or having your brains eaten by a horde of zombies.

Hardly a "bad" thing in those situations.

Conversely, excessive joy can lead to negative consequences too:

Think of someone experiencing a state of euphoria so intense, they lose empathy for other people's feelings and start unknowingly crossing their boundaries.

Or perhaps a bit closer to home: have you ever laughed so hard it hurt and you could barely breathe? Maybe been tickled to the point that you couldn't take it anymore?

Imagine feeling like that forever.

Suddenly "fun" doesn't seem like an exclusively "good" feeling anymore, does it?

What hurts is not the nature of the emotion, but the intensity.

Listening to a sad song can be a beautiful experience. And people willingly watch horror movies or go get angry on social media posts.

Why would we seek out those experiences if the emotions were inherently bad?

A perspective I've been playing with for the past years which feels deeply true to me is the idea that everything that exists is love viewed at different levels of obscurity.

When we look at emotions from that perspective, each feeling is simply a different flavor of love we get to experience.

Sweet tasting food is easier to appreciate than bitter or sour food.

But not learning to enjoy the latter flavors robs you of the opportunity to discover the richness that can be found in more complex and sophisticated foods.

Broadening your palate to all flavors, does great things for your life:

- It allows you to enjoy the food present wherever you are (not just in the candy shop).
- It leads to a more varied and balanced diet, which is healthier.
- It enhances your social experiences, as you get to share a wide range of meals together.

It is the same with emotions.

When you adapt your emotional palate to a wider range of feelings:

- You get to enjoy yourself, whatever your current emotional state is.
- You have a more varied and balanced experience of life, which makes you grow wiser.
- It enhances your social experiences, as you get to share a variety of interactions and dynamics with others.

"Good vibes only", is the equivalent of a dietary preference saying *"Birthday cakes only"*. It's enjoyable for a while, but it leads to problems down the line.

But I guess I'm moving a bit fast here. Let's rewind:

—*"Flavors of love, you say?*

I can entertain a lot of whacky ideas. But I don't see how rage, anxiety or depression could be forms of love."—

I understand it's hard to see the love within things that can be so painful or destructive.

But I think that's the point.

I believe love likes to play hide and seek.

Remember how we talked about the ocean before?

How the ocean gives rise to individual waves like you and I, and makes us believe we're separate from that greater whole until we collapse back into it, then delights in welcoming us back?

That's what love does. Love is the ocean?

It creates waves we call *"hate"* or *"judgment"* or *"apathy"* and makes us believe none of them are love.

Until we finally unmask them. Then it delights in someone having found out its true nature: That every wave is part of the same ocean. And even the darkest things —which appear impossible to reconcile with the whole— are still as much part of the ocean of love as you and I.

Sadness is love.

We feel sad when we experience a lack or a loss.

This includes physical losses (like a death, a breakup, or moving to another house).

But also abstract losses like loss of trust, loss of freedom and loss of youth. Even loss of identity.

Sadness is the voice of longing.

Sadness is the love for what is not —or is no longer— here.

Anger is love.

Because we only get angry when we truly care about something.

Even if sometimes that thing is ourselves, at the expense of everyone else.

Anger gives us the power to set boundaries and protect what we love.

Sometimes, we may project our anger on different people (or things) than what we *really* care about. And it can come up in ways that don't look pretty at all.

But it always originates from a form of care.

Even if it's just caring for oneself.

Fear is love.

Because it alerts us of potential threats to anything we love enough to want it to stay safe.

Whether it's our loved ones, our body, our ego or our bank account, fear is there to help us protect it.

It heightens our awareness and increases the possibilities available to us for helping what we love survive.

Instant fear makes you capable of running, fighting, playing dead or fawning in ways you normally wouldn't.

Creeping anxiety makes you capable of strategizing, anticipating, and coming up with unusual solutions for potential worst-case scenarios.

This too, is a form of love.

Even shame —one of the hardest emotions for many of us to enjoy— is an expression of love.

We feel shame when we think we've harmed others or did something that would cause others not to love us anymore.

Shame is a powerful force that wants to ensure our survival.

It's a force that can teach us how to get along with others —for better or worse.

Shame makes you capable of changing your behavior without requiring willpower.

It makes you want to *do* good, and *be* good, so that you may receive more love in the future or not get abandoned by the tribe.

So yes, by its very nature, high amounts of shame can be toxic.

But appropriate amounts of shame can keep you from pooping in your neighbor's front yard when you had too many tequilas.

Disgust is a force of love.

We feel disgust when our instincts tell us that something is no bueno.

While fear guards us from (things perceived as) imminent threats, disgust gives us the signal to stay away from something which might be contaminated or present a long-term danger.

This includes non-physical contamination, like being disgusted with the behavior of a group of people and urging you to stay away from them.

In other words: disgust is a (slightly unpleasant) form of self-care.

When someone asks *"Are you happy?"*, how do you know?

You might answer *"I just check if I feel good or not"*.

But I'd like you to consider that maybe happiness is something deeper:

It's loving, embracing and treasuring your life — moments of suffering, moments of fortune — and savoring all those experiences.

When I do this, happiness becomes like the background music to life.

I can be very angry but also happy.

It's one of the reasons music and art can make us so happy.

You cannot put your feelings into music while pushing that same feeling away.

By turning feelings into art, people celebrate every aspect of life.

And then they share it with others who are now also invited to embrace and celebrate it.

You don't need to be an artist to bring this concept of happiness into your life:

How you define happiness dictates how happy you get to be.

If your definition is narrow and tied to a specific emotional state, you'll only be happy when feeling that specific emotion.

The more possible experiences you include in your definition of happiness , the happier you become.

Which in turn changes the nature of those experiences.

We often speak of emotions as if they are states we can be *"in"*.

We'll say *"I'm going through a depression"* or *"I'm in a bad mood"*.

But that's not how emotions work.

Emotions are feelings moving *through you*.

You are not *in* a bad mood. A bad mood is in *you*.

You are the context in which the feelings arise.

Someone once told me I must be lying when I say I'm always happy.

They'd say *"I've seen you grumpy sometimes. So that's already proof you weren't happy."*

Or *"How can you be happy when there's so much suffering in the world? Doesn't that mean you're ignorant?"*

When you stop seeing happiness as an emotion and instead see it as an attitude of lovingly embracing what is, the question *"how can you be happy when this or that is happening?"* becomes obsolete.

Because the answer is always: By embracing it.

Embracing the thing, embracing the feelings that arise in response to it, and embracing any unwillingness to embrace those.

Who's doing that embracing? You.

And what's an embrace, if not an expression of love?

Love and happiness are commonly seen as feelings. But unlike other feeling states, like joy or excitement, they don't move through you. They are part of the context in which all other emotions move.

They are your nature.

Always there, welcoming each feeling as it passes through and succeeds the previous one.

Just as you are but a tiny wave expressed by the ocean, each emotion is but a tiny wave expressed inside *you*.

An infinite web of waves inside waves inside oceans inside oceans. All made of love.

Each drop of water is simultaneously a separate entity and inseparable from the whole.

Your cells might relate to the job they have in your body the way you relate to your own job in society, who knows?!

All I know is that from where I'm looking, emotions are waves of love that each come with their own unique flavor. And the more I'm willing to taste them, the more of the ocean's power is available to me.

And all I know is that from where I'm looking, you are a wave of love, coming with your own unique flavor.

A darn fine one, might I add...

So how much more of yourself are you willing to taste?

And how much more of your own nature might become available to you if you did?

"If you were okay with being unhappy, would you still be unhappy?"

- Naval Ravikant

CHAPTER 18
THE BIGGEST COSTUME PARTY IN THE WORLD

"You are the sun in drag.

You are God hiding from yourself.

Remove all the "mine"—that is the veil.

Why ever worry about

Anything?

Listen to what your friend Hafiz

Knows for certain:

The appearance of this world

Is a Magi's brilliant trick, though its affairs are

Nothing into nothing.

You are a divine elephant with amnesia

Trying to live in an ant

Hole.

Sweetheart, O sweetheart,

You are God in drag!"

— Hafiz

We seek outside ourselves.

And we seek outside of the here and now:

"If only I had this..."

"If only I had that..."

"If only I was a little more so and so..."

"...then surely, I'd be where I want to be!"

Possibly true?

Maybe so.

But the hypothetical is not where life is lived.

It's a virtual reality which has no impact on what's happening.

Sure, it can inspire your direction, but if you want to move from one situation to another, you have to use what's here. What's available to you at this moment.

Not what *could* be available in an alternate universe, inhabited by an alternate you.

Did you know the word "success" originated as the noun use of the past participle of the verb "succeed"?

Meaning *"to come after, follow after or take the place of"*?

Excuse all that nerd-speak, but what does it reveal?

We talked before about "destinations" not being real.

And success being as impermanent as anything else.

When we take success in its original meaning, success *is* impermanence.

Success *is* the journey even when it's mistaken for a destination.

Success is the noun of the past participle of the process of each moment following the previous one.

To be alive is to succeed over and over again.

So to seek success is merely to anticipate the continuation of life as it unfolds itself through you.

We seek answers.

And we seek certainty.

But certainty is a "destination". Certainty is when the process ends.

Certainty is death. Uncertainty is life.

Uncertainty is the nature of your current existence.

The more comfortable you become with uncertainty, the greater your capacity to feel alive.

Roller coasters make us feel alive.

A suspenseful movie. A great piece of music or the rapture of a passionate sexual interaction. These things make us feel deeply alive

Because we don't know what will happen at the next twist or turn.

Such is true about life at any moment.

What will happen in its next twist?

How will it make us feel?

We don't know, that's the truth of it.

Nothing is secure, but we love to pretend it is.

We predict and plan and theorize. Just enough until we feel we know the nature of life.

Just enough to think we know what we're doing and why.

Enough to believe we live in a world that is largely known to us, even though we've witnessed less than a millionth of a percentage of it.

The unknown is all there ever is.

The known is just a story we tell ourselves.

Direct experience can be known but is transient, as each moment is succeeded by the next.

The closest to a "known" is the eternal, ever-changing "now".

"Now" is the unknown being revealed, over and over.

The only way to find something is to encounter it.

The only place and time where things can be encountered is right here and now.

Yet when we don't encounter what we wish to, the first place we search is somewhere else.

"I'm sure it's out there somewhere!", we say.

When perhaps it would be more fitting to say *"I'm sure it's in here somewhere".*

Out there somewhere, is where we search.

But here, right now, is where we find.

So you could say that the very thing preventing you from finding is the act of searching.

Love, freedom, happiness, that important thing you had to remember but slipped your mind again; most of the things we seek in desperation can finally be found the moment we stop the search.

The search will be over when you stop searching.

You will have arrived the moment you start arriving.

You can find beauty in what's here when you don't fixate on what is not.

Most of the time what you seek is yourself, projected onto something else.

Love isn't out there for you to find.

Love is your nature.

Freedom is your nature.

Happiness, joy and clarity are your nature.

As long as you search, you won't be aware of this.

Because you won't be here.

Whenever you halt, you are here again. You become aware.

You are here now. Face yourself

You are the unknown being revealed.

You are love constantly rediscovering itself in a game of hide and seek.

You are God in drag, having the time of your life.

Attending the biggest costume party in the world.

Where everyone's masked and everything's decorated.

So committed to the fun that we're fully immersed in our characters.

CHAPTER 19
ENDLESS GAMES OF HIDE AND SEEK

"Count 1 to 10 without a peek
You go hide! And then I seek!
Where'd you go? Where'd you hide?
You're not in the places I tried!
I look over here, I look over there.
I look up and down and everywhere!
You're good at this, where did you go?
Are you here? yes, yes, yes....no!"

— Nursery Rhyme

I told you I believe love likes to play hide and seek.

I find proof of that wherever I go.

Because I've rarely met a person who doesn't have the spark of love in their eyes when given the chance to show it.

Despite all our radiant magnificence, it's surprisingly uncommon for people to recognize that spark in themselves.

We look up and down and everywhere. We see the love in other people (or the love we believe they could give to us). We see the love in a perfect piece of art or a perfect strand of DNA.

We find the love at the bottom of a bottle or in a tub of Ben & Jerry's.

We project it onto other people's bosoms but we fail to feel it in our own.

And there's a part of me that sees this as a tremendous tragedy. That sees the suffering it perpetuates for ourselves and others. But maybe, just maybe...that's the game love likes to play.

If at all times of the day each and every one of us fully realized we were God in drag, what would there be left to do?

If we never forgot our own divinity we could never be delighted by its discovery. We would no longer seek to find love in other things. And we might stop interacting with them altogether.

Because most people who *do* find their heart overflowing with love feel compelled to let it spill over on those around them. To do something that contributes to the healing of humanity.

But what if everyone else was already overflowing with love too?

There'd we'd all be. No needs or desires left to fulfill in ourselves or others. No "problems" to overcome. Nothing to heal. Nothing left to learn or discover.

Just a bunch of waves spilling out onto each other, forming one singular ocean.

Enjoying our own existence for eternity.

As I'm writing this, I chuckle.

Because I was trying to show how uninteresting it would be if we'd all be whole and healed.

But as the words poured onto this paper, it started to seem like a beautiful hypothetical happy ending.

Here's the thing though: Happy endings only feel so good because of the contrast created by what came before them.

Without a bit of tension or drama leading up to it, there isn't even a story to enjoy in the first place.

Imagine a movie trailer that says:

"This summer, experience the adventure of a lifetime.

Our protagonist was born happy.

From that moment on, they remained happy.

Coming soon to theaters near you."

Would you camp out in front of the theater to be the first to watch it?

Personally, I wouldn't.

Because nothing would happen.

I might as well sit with myself in silence.

In the 2002 movie "The Bourne Identity", a man wakes up on a beach with amnesia.

He tries to remember who he is but all he finds are fragments.

Meanwhile he continuously has to protect himself from threats and attacks.

He falls in love with a woman named Marie, who becomes an essential ally in uncovering the truth about his identity.

Now that's an enticing plot!

What if love hides itself in human forms so that it too gets the opportunity to witness an exciting story from time to time? To experience what it's like not to have the happy ending yet?

That would explain a lot of things.

Like why do the humans who long for love the deepest behave exactly in the ways that sabotage them from finding it?

Why do we run away from the places we're most likely to find love? Or put up barriers so that we can't feel it when we're close to it?

Why does finding wholeness feel like such a journey for most people?

There's plenty of nuanced perspectives to answer that.

I invite you to consider this one:

Love likes playing hide and seek.

It's hiding inside you.

And sometimes, when it's having a little too much fun, it doesn't want to be found out yet.

Because that would mean the game's over.

So if you catch yourself in patterns of recurring drama, or desperate yearnings or dating people who aren't good to you, see if you can step back.

Maybe even have a laugh at how love skilfully managed to escape itself again.

What an exciting game!

Then have a knock on the door of your heart.

Talk to love directly:

"I know you're in there, buddy!"

Close your eyes.

Count to 10.

And yell:

"Ready or not, here I come..."

Love plays hide and seek the way a blue sky does.

It never really goes anywhere to hide. It just obscures itself.

One day that may look like spotty white clouds: You see the blue sky is there but the clouds change your impression of it.

Other days the sky can be so overcast with darkness that you don't even think of the fact that underneath it all, it's bright blue.

There's even days when the sky thunders and roars and sets entire forests on fire with bursts of electricity. Yet underneath it all, it's still that same blue sky

It's easy to recognize love when it hides inside empathy, bliss or forgiveness.

That's the equivalent of a child hiding behind a transparent curtain.

Gotcha!

But when it's hidden inside darker emotions like arrogance, fear or grief, it becomes harder to spot.

Still, I believe all these emotions are flavors of love in one way or another.

The sky that's blue is the same sky that's thundering. Just with a different flavor.

Some emotions can feel so dark and intense that love becomes almost unrecognizable in their disguise.

It's hard to look at apathy, despair or humiliation and see the love within them.

Yet like the blue sky behind the darkest thunderstorms, the love behind these feelings didn't leave, it's only more obscured.

One might humiliate another person in a twisted attempt to place themselves above them. Cause that's the only way they feel they can catch a brief recognition of their self-love.

Another person could become completely apathetic as some dark way of welcoming and embracing life as it is. In which they sacrifice their own needs and boundaries to create something which resembles loving acceptance, but through the mechanism of bracing in collapse rather than embracing with open chest.

You could say that the darker someone's emotional state gets; the harder it is for them to see the love inside and outside of them.

It's like playing hide and seek on hard mode.

On the other hand, the brighter the feeling, the more fully we become aware of love.

Most cloudy skies still show a hint of blue, and most of love's disguises still contain a visible clue of its identity.

A golden thread to follow in the labyrinth.

Love wants to be found, so it gently invites us to find more and more of it.

And the more we find love, the more of it we continue to find.

Until at some point, if we followed the golden thread all the way out of the maze, love becomes the only thing we see.

But when love hides under enough obscurity, those clues are no longer obvious.

That's when the hide and seek game starts to resemble a tragedy.

When we feel an emotion dark enough to make us forget our own nature, we lose integrity. We start to play the game at the cost of each other

The question *"Where do I find love?"* is no longer a curiosity but it has become a lack. A need.

Now we start seeing others as opportunities to have it fulfilled, rather than continuing to see them as they are.

That is how objectification happens. That's how we stop seeing people as people, but start seeing them as prospective clients, opportunities to get laid or one of the roles that we put them in (like "boyfriend", "boss" or "barista").

This is the threshold at which love has hidden itself so well, it no longer remembers its own location. It starts to panic and grasp on to others, hoping it can find itself through them.

At this point, the golden thread is lost. And instead, it's the darkness that calls us.

Luring us in with the illusion that —if love is so hard to find— we must keep looking in dark corners to find it.

It's when we follow this call of darkness, instead of patiently looking for the golden thread, that we descend and spiral down.

What was once a need or a lack projected onto others, now becomes desperation. And what was once mild objectification turns into the desire to control and dominate people into satisfying our needs.

What was once an occasional lie or trick to reach a favorable outcome now turns into abuse and political power games.

Yet underneath all this behavior is somehow still that blue sky of love trying to find itself.

Completely unaware that it's looking at a mirror.

Just as one might follow the golden thread all the way up to the sun, to emotions like bliss, peace or ecstacy where love's all-encompassing light becomes so apparent that we might even forget we ever believed anything else existed, it's possible to descend into darkness all the way down to a point where it feels like there's little left to conclude than that love never existed in the first place and black is the true color of the sky.

This is where we find perpetual states of guilt, nihilism and unworthiness.

At this point love is so obscured, that rather than thinking we can (ab)use others to find it, we no longer believe it can be found at all.

Such intense states of darkness can have a gravitational pull to them.

Tempting you with defeatist thoughts like:

- *"Why are you still doing this?"*
- *"Isn't it about time you give up?"*
- *"Does anything matter at all?"*

But if such thoughts should ever befall you, don't be fooled.

Love's still playing hide and seek with you.

Testing the persistence of your faith that it *is* indeed waiting to be found by you.

And it didn't just take the bus home while you were counting down for the hide and seek game.

Love is waiting to cheer for you when you find it.

Ready to lift you up from the moment you reunite.

Ready to take you to unseen heights.

Celebrating every step of the way as you get closer to finding it fully.

It will cheer for you when you think you see it in someone else.

Because even though that's only part of the truth, it's not entirely false either.

Each time you find a piece of love somewhere, it will lift you up a little more. It will continue to delight in playing this game with you and drop a few clues where to find its next part.

Hoping that maybe one day, you'll find it everywhere all at once all the time.

Love is seeking itself inside all of us.

When people are in integrity, love seeks itself within and gives what it finds outwardly.

Low-integrity behavior happens when it seeks outwardly and we try to extract energy from others in an attempt to fill the gaping hole we believe exists inside of us.

For love to be infinite and boundless, evil has to exist.

Despite all the grief it causes, it can't *not* exist without placing limitations on the forms love can take on.

Pure evil exists as the experiential reality of love being 100% absent.

Pure love exists as the opposite of that —love being 100% present.

So the darker our emotional state, the darker our behavior becomes.

And the darker our behavior, the harder it can be to eventually face ourselves.

It's still relatively easy to forgive yourself for lying to avoid pain. Or using some manipulative tactics to get your needs met. But once people start hating and shaming themselves, it pushes them further into obscurity.

The resulting behavior becomes increasingly dark and hard to forgive for most people.

At some point, it starts involving conscious disrespect of boundaries. Or acts of coercion and physical violence.

Some people slip into behavior so dark it reaches a place which can seem "unforgivable".

In extreme cases, awareness of love can be so gravely obscured that the only way to feel it is to take it from a being so obviously innocent they're guaranteed to have love within them.

Such acts may seem unthinkable but when we follow the seduction of darkness instead of the golden thread love left for us, you'd be surprised how easily our morals can shift.

For example:

What starts as a mild feeling of disgust for people with different values can fall down a slippery slope into things like racism or homophobia before we catch ourselves.

The tragedy is that even for these most terrible acts, the emotion behind them did contain a golden thread of love, which wasn't followed because the pull of the darkness was stronger.

What begins as a deep-seated love for one's own tribe, can evolve into a preservation instinct, manifesting as disgust for the "other",. Ultimately escalating to the dehumanization and attempted elimination of an entire group of people.

Suddenly people who had never any intention to cause harm, contribute to a genocide.

This is not to say *"mass murder is OK, it's all love"*. On the contrary. It's to urge you to find the love wihin all feelings you experience, so that none might ever tempt you further into darkness.

And to find compassion for those who haven't found a glimpse of love yet.

Whichever feeling state you are currently in, or whatever part of you you are judging/not welcoming, know that you can find the golden thread of love within.

No matter how obscured, the love is there.

Follow it and you will find your way back home.

— *"Why though?*

We get it, love likes playing hide and seek.

But why do so many have to suffer for it?

Why does there have to be so much destruction and injustice in the world?" —

I can't claim to know the answer to that.

What I can tell you is that when I notice the "why" question come up in my mind, what hides behind is usually the longing for love as well.

Love in the form of wanting myself to feel safer by understanding my environment better.

Or in the form of wanting to be more able to embrace it all.

Behind my "why" questions is the illusion that if I somehow got an answer, a reasonable explanation of causality, something that I can logically understand and react to with *"Oh, yeah, I guess that makes sense"*, that it would make painful things easier to accept.

But as a wise **drunk** guy once told me:

"When you've finally found the root cause of all issues...how will that help you?

You'll still be right where you are now.

Either having to accept it, or to take some kind of action."

One day, I asked love the question:

"Why do so many people have to suffer?"

In response, I saw a visual memory of myself at five years old.

Joyfully jumping on a sandcastle I had spent all afternoon sculpting.

Could it be that for us, tiny little waves, terrible things like volcanic eruptions and countries torn apart by wars are very, very real, but that to the ocean of life it's just play?

The same way that stories you played out with your toys as a kid could have felt very intense for the toys?

Especially if those toys would have believed they were separate beings, rather than just physical objects being moved by your mind as you played out your fun little story with them.

I guess it's a matter of perspective.

And as humans, our perspective will naturally gravitate to that of the human in the story.

Not that of life as a whole.

Love is infinite and unconditional.

And the only way for love to be both is to love its own infinite forms. Including the ones that aren't always pretty.

- Cute little puppies
- Spontaneous cuddle puddles
- Your neighbor bringing you freshly baked apple pie still warm from the oven

Those are easy to love.

But if love wasn't able to experience the totality of human suffering and love it too, it would be less loving than it is.

It wouldn't be itself anymore.

That's the paradox:

If love didn't love hatred, there would be less love and more hatred.

Of course, this doesn't mean we can engage in hatred and call it love.

That would be disowning our own nature.

Remember:

Our darkest emotions are the result of love *not* recognizing itself.

"Forgiveness is just another name for freedom."

— Byron Katie

This is a book on living as you are.

And what you *are not* are your emotions or thoughts.

You are the space those things happen in.

However, it's fairly common for humans to end up holding on to some of the emotions that pass through.

There are many reasons we might do so, ranging from identification to trauma to things beyond the scope of this book.

Three of those reasons —all very similar in nature— are grudges, resentments and regrets.

In essence, all three of them arise from an unwillingness to forgive something that happened.

We hold on to a feeling (for example: anger or shame), and tell ourselves we won't let it pass until what happened has been atoned for by whomever we hold accountable for it.

As long as this feeling is held on to, it will at times act as an impediment to being who you are.

If someone hurt you, and you now want to hurt them back in revenge, you've been infected with their darkness.

If someone's angry behavior pisses you off: you've been infected with their rage

If someone's racism makes you dehumanize them ("they're just a bigot"), you've been infected with their ignorance.

Their pain wasn't yours to feel.

Yes, you did get to feel it, and that might not have been your choice. But you don't need to hold on to it and make it a part of you.

This doesn't mean you should be tolerant of abuse and indignities. But it's an invitation not to continue those things inside yourself.

To find the golden thread that whomever did this thing couldn't find in their feeling at the time, and use it to forgive within whatever capacity you have.

Because when you forgive someone (including yourself), it is you who are relieved. It is you who are set free. You get to be yourself again, instead of being a puppet for the grudge.

Forgive more.

Not to let people off the hook, but to break the cycle.

The history books are filled with horrors perpetrated by people who felt justified by their own victimization.

Forgiveness is healing.

If you can't find it in your heart to forgive someone, don't do it yet.

Yes, it's true that this grudge is not you. But it is you who's holding onto it.

As long as that is still what you want, forgiveness won't be available.

Waiting is.

Fake forgiveness would be as useless as fake apologies.

Because it comes at the expense of the self.

Be as you are.

If right now that means holding on to resentment, then hold on to it.

There might come a day when it weighs too heavy to keep holding, or there may never.

Like a wise stoner once said:

"It's all good bro!"

You don't need to be like Jesus or Buddha or Krishna (of course, you can if you really want to). Who came up with such a torturous idea? To expect ourselves to behave in a way so uncommon for humans that we still speak of the few who did so thousands of years later?

It's beautiful to have aspirations, inspirations and role models. And if these don't match reality yet, well, that's kinda how aspirations work.

In the meantime, be yourself as you are now. Look for the humility in that.

Forgive yourself and others within the capacity you have today.

And with each grudge, resentment or regret you let go of, you'll find more of yourself becomes available to you.

CHAPTER 20
OPENING AND CLOSING TO LOVE

Love is an embracing, welcoming energy.

So the more we can embrace and welcome what's happening — events, feelings, sensations, thoughts— the more we'll arrive in a state of love.

By embracing an experience, we help love find itself inside it.

The more we help love find itself in its most challenging games of hide and seek, the more we rediscover happiness as the stable undercurrent to all our experiences.

If you're wondering whether we went on some weird, abstract detour here: this is 100% relevant to any pursuit of personal development.

Because until you find love, happiness and a sense of security, the majority of your goals will be projections of your own longing for them.

Some of those goals may require a huge amount of effort to achieve. While the necessity of achieving them could disappear if you were to wholeheartedly join love in its current game of hide and seek.

What was once a huge project, can now be replaced by the practice of embracing what's happening and finding the love in it.

Once you have practiced this for a while, and you've found the undercurrent of happiness that is the stage all your other emotions dance on, your goals and desires are free to be expressions of the love within you, rather than attempts to extract it from something external.

Pre-happiness goals are often attempts to control life. To manipulate it into treating us a certain way.

Post-happiness goals are more like acts of play. Improvised dances or gifts to the world.

Their intention is not to trick life into giving you anything.

The intention of post-happiness goals is to explore, expand and share the love that's already found.

These goals feel different.

The tension around them melts away. And you gain access to a type of creativity not available when there's a contraction or a holding on to that desired outcome.

As long as the outcome of a goal is perceived as your ticket to love and happiness, there will be a neediness about achieving.

This blocks a lot of your natural creativity. Because creativity thrives in the irrational, the risky and the nonlinear.

To some people, the above can sound like having pre-happiness goals is "bad" and having post-happiness goals is "good".

But that would be quite an unloving way to look at those pre-happiness goals.

After all, if a goal's intention is for you to feel more loved, secure or happy, then what else is that goal but an expression of the loving care you already feel for yourself?

In an utopian world, we'd all feel loved, healed and whole all the time. From the moment we were born.

But we don't choose our childhoods or the amount of times in life we encounter tragedy and malice.

It's rare to meet a human who hasn't encountered some form of trauma in their lives. And some would say being born in itself is a traumatic event.

To me, most of life feels like a process of walking each other home to wholeness.

Like that's part of the point of being here.

We each get dropped at a different starting point in this game of hide and seek.

Little waves emerging from the ocean of love.

Playing our own little games of hide and seek. Not realizing how connected we are to everything.

Carrying each other home as we impact each other with our movements.

Trying to figure out where we come from, where we're going and how the hedge we'll get there.

So I guess it's normal that we spend a significant amount in confusion and misdirection.

Wouldn't that be the case for anyone who's navigating without knowing where they started or what the destination is?

Wouldn't someone in such a situation also latch on to every other human they run into that might help them find the way?

Or fall for illusions just to give them something to hold on to? Something that can at least make them feel they know where they are?

Just like a dehydrated traveler in the desert would steal, kill or beg for a drop of water, or spend all their energy chasing an oasis only to find out it was a mirage, chasing the mirages of pre-happiness goals (or resorting to non-integrous behavior and trying to use others for our survival) is a normal part of the process for most of us.

Pre-happiness goals are the goals of dehydrated travelers. And dehydrated travelers aren't bad people with faulty goals. They're regular people; with very appropriate goals for what they're experiencing at that moment.

What I'm trying to say is: If you're currently unhappy or find that all your goals feel like desperate needs, then yes: Those goals are probably projections.

And yes: Many of them will be mirages too.

...but also, yes: You don't have to feel ashamed for having them. They might be exactly what you need right now.

Just know that, if you manage to do so, finding the love inside what's already here might be an easier way home.

If you currently can't find the love within what's happening (or the love for who you are), the one thing I'd caution you for is to not force yourself to find it.

Don't override your true present experience with some phrase from this book that sounds good.

Trust your own pace.

Trust that what you feel has meaning and relevance right now.

Just like forcing someone to make love to you is *absolutely not* an act of love, forcing yourself to be grateful for something you're unhappy with is not an act of gratitude.

Forcing yourself to repeat the idea that everything is love —when currently to you it feels like suffering— is not an act of love either.

Those are acts of self-denial, which paradoxically, make it harder to feel love.

The fastest path to love is embracing what's here now.

So that means if you currently don't have the capacity or willingness to embrace a certain aspect of what's here, then the fastest path to love is to embrace that you don't.

And with embrace, I don't mean "See it as a shortcoming which you accept". But to recognize it is not a shortcoming in the first place.

That we are all here to be human and that love knows no hierarchies.

Love is not a competition. Love is just here for you.

Sometimes you'll feel a lot of it. Other times just a little.

But feeling one thing doesn't make you superior to feeling another.

Just like sleeping isn't worse than being awake or night isn't worse than day.

Sure, it's harder to go to work when you're asleep and it's harder to be calm when you're upset. But the issue isn't that working is better than sleeping or calm is better than anger, it's that when we believe we should be in a different state than the one we are in right now, we postpone our natural return home.

Because remember:

You can't go anywhere without starting where you are.

Emotions are adaptive energies meant to move us towards action in four stages:

1. They give us information about our environment (like identifying a threat, or a source of pleasure)

2. They create a physiological response, preparing our body to handle this information (like the surge of anxiety you feel when a velociraptor appears in your living room — or how your genitals feel funny each time that attractive barista takes your order)

3. They move you towards the action (like punching that velociraptor in the face —or telling the barista you no longer need the espresso because they already made your heart beat faster and their beauty makes you feel warmer than any cup of coffee could)

4. The feeling subsides

That means each time you feel an emotion move through you, its intended conclusion is some kind of action, followed by the emotion disappearing.

Sadness may move you towards self-care and rest. Or towards connection by sharing your feelings and needs with others.

Anger can move you towards taking a stand, making clear decisions, or initiating radical changes in your life.

If you allow the emotions to move you towards that final act (provided of course the act doesn't involve harming others), the natural result is you get to experience the love within it.

For example:

- Feeling depressed, cuddling up with a blanket and snacks, while watching your favorite childhood movie...and suddenly finding some joy in that.

- Being so angry you break up with your partner or quit your job... and feeling empowered that you finally chose what's best for yourself.

But when we buy into the culturally prescribed idea that certain emotions are "bad", what will happen instead is this:

As soon as they come up (in stage 1 or 2), we'll suppress them.

The issue with that is not so much that the action from stage 3 didn't happen (after all, those actions are often not appropriate to the situation).

The issue is that the emotion wasn't allowed to fully pass through your body because in order to stop it from leading to the action, we had to physically hold back that energy.

On a surface level, this may feel like we successfully kept the emotion at bay. But what actually happens is this:

1. The emotion perpetually continues to try and move us towards completing its final stages.

2. To suppress that, our body expends an equal amount of energy stopping that action from happening.

Think of how much energy it costs your body to hold back a drunk friend from making a dumb decision. That's the same amount of energy it takes our bodies to hold ourselves back from an action our emotions want us to take.

This has three consequences:

1. Because it costs so much to stop feeling the emotion, "just living life" becomes more exhausting.

2. The mechanism of suppression doesn't discriminate: Either you numb yourself down and block all emotions or you open up and allow them all. You can't just suppress sadness, fear and anger while continuing to feel joy. Your joy will be suppressed as well.

3. Like holding a beach ball underwater, the more we push down on the emotion, the more it pushes back. The pressure is growing and growing. Until eventually, it becomes too much to contain, and the (by now exaggerated) emotion *will* successfully complete its journey. Which it may do at a very inopportune moment.

That last point is especially important because it can have a big impact on your relationships with others.

Let's say one day you got angry and wanted to stand up for yourself (an act of love).

But you didn't, for whatever reason (let's say it involved punching your boss in the face, but you kinda liked your job and your spotless criminal record so you chose not to).

At some point you'll still have to release that energy somehow, because the emotion still wants to pass.

As long as you don't do that, continued suppression is required to go on with your day.

If you successfully suppress the anger for long enough, you'll no longer be aware of it.

But it will still be there.

When you push back against an emotion you feel, how could it ever pass?

It's like barricading the exit of your house, then telling your visitors to leave.

Just like your visitors would start looking for alternative escape routes, your locked up emotions will be looking for opportunities to complete their 3-stage trajectory. And this can take many forms:

- Having a "short fuse" or "chip on your shoulder"
- Constantly thinking others are mistreating you or being mistreated (as a way to give you an excuse to be angry)
- Experiencing a mild annoyance about everything (allowing little bits and pieces of the anger to complete their journey, one at a time)
- Sarcasm and passive-aggressive communication (leaking little bits of anger into each conversation)
- Joining a positive cause and protesting it as a subconscious outlet for rage

What's interesting about all these examples is that none of them resemble love any more.

Getting into fights with strangers is certainly not an act of love.

But it's still the result of a suppressed emotion which originally *intended* to move you into an act of self-love (standing up for yourself).

That original emotion is still there. But after all the suppression, it comes out in some twisted, perverted or toxic way.

Just look at many priests: Repressing their sexual emotions for a lifetime, until one day...

Needless to say, perverted priest behavior is not what we are aiming for in life.

Why do these feelings come out in such twisted ways? And not just in the original way?

I believe it does because suppression is the act of closing ourselves off to love.

(Of course, in one sense, suppression itself is just another flavor of love. As it protects us from things we don't want to feel. But let's not get too meta here).

When love speaks to us in the form of an emotion which we don't want to feel (or which we wisely choose not to express because we don't want to harm ourselves or others), we have to find a way to stop listening.

So we push that feeling, that particular expression of love, into a temporary hiding place. Some dark corner, where it can't be recognized.

And since it loves playing hide and seek, it willingly obliges. But of course, it does so expecting us to eventually go search for it again.

So if we forget where we hid it, it'll keep screaming louder and louder until we can't help but pay attention.

Now obscured by darkness, it might indeed do so in very "unloving" ways.

Because as we've seen: when love gets desperate, things can get quite dark indeed.

But (at this point), its real desire isn't to harm others for harm's sake. It's merely acting in more extreme ways so that it can finally be found again.

Luckily, as we're about to see, we are always surrounded by allies that can help us find where it hides.

When we interact with each other, the old emotions inside us that long to complete their journey are often brought up to surface.

This is what it means to get triggered.

We see being triggered as bad because it often manifests as rage, blame and disconnect. But from the perspective of every emotion being a flavor of love —and love constantly playing games of hide and seek— being triggered can be seen as love stepping out of its hiding place, saying:

"Look at me, here I am, still hiding in plain sight, teasing you relentlessly...

Can you find me this time?"

In this way, every moment in which we're triggered is a prime opportunity to find love back.

By asking: *"What's happening here? What is this feeling wanting to be felt?"* and then, rather than blaming the other for our feeling, welcoming and embracing the feeling itself.

Until you find the love within.

I have been deeply happy for about a decade. But there still seems to be no shortage of unprocessed stuff inside me.

The only difference is that now when it comes up, I have the capacity to be with it (or I'm surrounded by people who can lend me some of theirs).

Capacity is the keyword in all of this. Because on paper, finding the love and happiness inside things is easy.

You just say: *"I'll embrace what's happening, no matter how painful or terrifying it seems."*

But in practice, that isn't always as easy as it sounds.

If you don't have the capacity to embrace a thing without it completely overwhelming your nervous system, welcoming it is not going to lead you towards a state of love.

Instead, it might lead you to a state of overwhelm.

And that's what happens to many of us as kids: We are faced with experiences so painful or scary that there's no way for our system to process them, let alone find that golden thread of love inside the darkness.

So we go into overwhelm and find a way not to have to be with this experience anymore.

This suppression of (or dissociation from) feelings can be seen as closing ourselves to love, and the embracing or welcoming of them as opening ourselves to it.

Because of love's constant longing to find itself, we might think by default that "opening to love" is the superior choice.

But remember: Whether we are opening or closing, we are doing so indiscriminately. We either open ourselves to every flavor of love, or none of it.

So check in with yourself. Open at your own pace.

Increase your capacity little by little.

Because if you overwhelm yourself by opening too much too fast, the only natural conclusion will be a knee-jerk closing response like suppression or dissociation.

I do believe every experience in life can be received as a gift on our journey.

But some gifts take a few more years (or decades) to unwrap than others.

In hindsight, most of the people I once saw as villains in my story, were giving me the seeds or catalysts for big positive transformation. They too were guiding me home. And all of them did contribute to my growth once I was ready to process those experiences.

Still, a lot of it incapacitated me for years.

Yes, whatever painful experience comes your way *can* be alchemized into pure love. But we'll all do so at a pace that comes natural to us.

And sometimes, that'll mean guarding ourselves from experiencing it at all.

Or having to lean on others as we spend time regaining our own capacity.

Eventually letting the experience metabolize slowly in little bites over a long period.

Each new trigger feeding us a new bite.

"There is only one way to eat an elephant: a bite at a time."

— Desmond Tutu

Emotions are often called irrelevant, when they are, in fact, highly relevant.

Some people might say: *"The fear you feel in this situation is holding you back. It's not what you need."* or *"The anger you feel about this small thing is entirely misplaced."*

And that's partly true: the thing we direct the expression of those feelings at is often not the cause of them.

But the feeling itself is always relevant.

As we've seen, most of us carry around unprocessed emotions.

Some are the result of biting your tongue at a corporate meeting or an awkward family dinner.

Others may be part of those big elephant-sized feelings we still carry with us from earlier trauma.

We don't feel all these feelings all the time. Suppression (and its unconscious cousin "repression") helps us keep them in the dark.

When we get triggered, we might be told that our feelings aren't relevant.

"It's just trauma. It has nothing to do with this situation."

And again, that's partly true: Whatever we are experiencing during a trauma response was not originally caused by what's happening right in front of us.

But the actual emotion coming up is *always* relevant. In fact, it is so relevant *because* it is trauma.

Trauma is what happens when we run into an experience that is too overwhelming for us to embrace.

Trauma is love. It protects us.

It helps us run, fight, dissociate, change personalities. It does whatever is needed for us not to crumble in the face of what's happening.

So if you panic, freeze, fawn or rage in response to a seemingly small thing, that feeling is not irrelevant. It is trying to protect you from going through a situation similar to the one that could've crumbled you at the time.

And there's a second reason why "old traumatic feelings" are so relevant:

They point you to parts of your history that still want to be embraced.

Like a sprained ankle that was never tended to and now occasionally makes it harder for you to functionally move as an athlete, trauma is a sprained piece of your emotional body making it harder for you to function in the emotional world.

Both are injuries created by past events. And if untreated, both will occasionally let you know not to forget that they need some attention.

It may come at unfortunate moments (then again, when would be a fortunate moment for it?), but like all emotions, it can help guide you and it's an expression of love wanting to be found again.

Not a dysfunction, but something very functional, that is often looked at with unloving eyes.

Most of our so-called "unhelpful" or "unloving" patterns, saved our sanity at some point.

If they're still keeping you safe from something you're not ready to handle just yet, don't force healing just because people say you should.

Don't shame yourself into embracing some terrible experience as a "gift" or a "form of love" just because that's what I told you in this book.

Yes, I'd love it for you if some of these ideas can act as little seeds that grow into big love for you someday. But if there's only one of them you take with you, let it be this:

Trust your own pace with infinite patience.

We have at least a lifetime to find the love within all that was given to us.

And if you'd force yourself to embrace the things that feel like too much for you, well, then you'd be forgetting to embrace yourself.

So it doesn't matter what some writer who's never met you has to say about the love hiding inside everything that hurt you.

The best person to assess how much of each emotion or behavior you are ready to embrace right now is you.

(And, let me tell you a secret:

There's plenty of stuff this writer hasn't found the capacity to embrace yet himself. He's just conveniently not writing about that.)

Have you ever loved someone who didn't love you back?

While such an experience still has plenty of love in it, which you clearly feel inside your heart, it's mostly signified by isolation and pain.

Maybe even a sense that the other person never truly saw or received what you were giving them. A sense of that love being taken for granted instead of fully felt.

When love is mutual however, it's almost as if that feeling expands every time you are together.

I've found this to be a powerful metaphor for how we relate to our emotions.

If an emotion comes to visit me but I reject it...how will I be able to receive its love?

On the other hand, if I practice welcoming each emotion and actively loving it, then I am creating the beautiful experience of mutual love between me and that emotion.

Instead of getting angry and wishing I wasn't feeling so, I say:

"Oh, there's some anger coming up... It must be that it thinks I could use some extra energy to dedicate to something I care about!"

So I welcome the anger and receive its gifts.

When I notice the urge to suppress it, I try to relax my body and eliminate distractions.

To hear what the anger is trying to tell me.

"What is it urging me to do? And how can I do so in a non-violent way?

Do I need to make some tough decisions? Set a boundary? Clean the house?"

I still have a strong preference for the emotions I was taught to label as good.

But I'm consciously practicing to let go of that.

And while I'd rather feel joy all the time, I've come to recognize four things:

1. Without emotions like anger, shame or fear, my joy would be quite dysfunctional. I'd just be joyfully taken advantage of, joyfully pushed aside and joyfully give all my money and energy to people who prey on the ignorant.

2. When I allow emotions to fully pass through my body, all emotions lead me back to joy anyway. That's the 4th stage of the emotion: It subsides and what remains is the under-current of happiness. But in the process, they all have a lot of wisdom, power and love to offer, if I allow myself to receive them.

3. Sweet food is easy to enjoy. And complex flavors can be hard to palate for an untrained tongue. But over time, experienced eaters develop a taste for such nuanced delicacies as they are more sensory stimulating. Similarly, joy is only one flavor of love, and the more of these emotions I learn to fully feel, the greater my capacity to experience love becomes.

4. As an extension of the latter, the love in myself also grows. Think of it this way: If you can only love your partner when they're in one specific mood, do you really love them? The more emotions I learn to love within myself, the more love I'm giving to myself (and receiving, obviously).

Since suppression as a mechanism doesn't discriminate, and the final stage of each emotion is joy or love, the depth of joy and happiness you are able to feel in life is in direct proportion to the amount of suffering you are willing to endure.

Suppressed emotions are held back by the body.

So are any emotions we choose to hold on to, like grudges.

They can manifest in our bodies as either tightly clenched muscles or as numb areas: Parts of our body we don't feel.

In this sense, what we suppress is what we become. Until we finally let the feeling pass.

What happens when you relax your awareness into those tight, painful or awkward places inside you?

When you take a moment to welcome what's there without judging it?

What if you try to explore which areas of your body you don't feel often and spend some time trying to feel them more deeply?

Each time you do this, you gently increase your capacity to feel yourself.

The more capacity you have to feel yourself, the more capacity you have to feel anything else.

Because the way we feel experiences is through the impact they have on us.

The more you feel of yourself and the impact things have on you, the more you can understand, express and align your life with who you really are.

There's only one caveat :

If you "feel it to heal it", you're one foot out the door.

Because this intention leads to feeling it while hoping doing so will stop you from having to.

No. Feel it to *feel* it. Get curious about your experience. Become a sommelier of the infinite flavors of love.

And you might even find that some of the things you were trying to learn to "tolerate" more become things you occasionally appreciate in moderation.

After all, if listening to a sad song can be a beautiful experience, then who says listening to your own sadness can't be beautiful from time to time?

Sleep gives you more energy during the day and daytime activity makes you more restful at night.

Alternating cycles of work and rest are what maximize your capacity for both.

Alternating cycles of social events and solitude maximize your presence for being with yourself and others.

In the same way, opening your heart to feelings isn't superior to closing it. It's the natural rhythms of opening and closing that maintain your capacity for welcoming and embracing what arises.

Your capacity to open yourself to love depends on your capacity to close yourself if needed.

The stronger your boundaries, the more you can let people get close to you without risking abuse.

I'm saying all this, because the human mind loves to make sense of the world by saying *"this is better than that"* or *"this option is good and its opposite is bad"*.

We've just had a long conversation about the idea that there is love hidden inside every experience if we are willing to fully be with it.

That conversation in itself was meant to liberate us from self-help platitudes like *"positive thinking"*, *"good vibes only"* and the idea that some emotions are to be avoided.

But the mind being the way it is, it's possible that it now starts seeing *"finding the love within"* as superior to *"not finding the love within"*.

So I want to clarify that this was not my intention, but a potential byproduct of the limitations of words.

Just like sleep is necessary for wakefulness, *"not finding the love"* and *"finding the love"* are both equally important aspects of the game of hide and seek.

Without something being hidden, we would never have the chance to find it.

Just like without death existing, it would not be possible for anyone to be alive.

On one level, discussing all this isn't necessary.

You (and everyone else) will always do what you want to do anyway.

So why write about any of this?

Because all of it requires a lot less effort when you do it with full awareness:

As part of these natural cycles, there will always be situations and periods in which you close yourself. And in those periods all connections will be lessened (to yourself, to others, to your intuition, to reality).

Because feeling less means hearing less of what everything inside and outside of you is telling you.

And yes, that means it will be harder to hear the soundtrack of happiness in your life.

You might find yourself chasing goals or habits that are illusions and projections.

But from a broader perspective, in such a period that is exactly what you need. Because it's only by realizing you were looking for love in illusions that the cycle re-starts and you get to find it in reality again. Just as you can only wake up by realizing you were sleeping or dreaming.

So in a period where you're closed down, depressing, or numbing yourself to avoid feeling your feelings, to outsiders it may seem like you're doing the wrong thing.

Which is funny. because they wouldn't say *"It's bad to take painkillers when recovering from a broken arm"*. Then why is it bad to go through a phase of numbing the pain when you're recovering from a broken heart?

Sure, eventually, you want to go back to opening to love. But if deep-rest is what you need for a while, or if numbing is what helps you recover as you slowly build up capacity to feel again, then embrace it.

Just don't go so far down the stairs of darkness that you don't find the golden thread anymore.

That's the reason why we went on this whole detour:

Yes, the core message of this book is to just allow yourself to be. And to allow yourself to do what it is that you want to do most right now.

Even if it seems nonsensical or "wrong".

But just like when we dream, we don't realize we're awake (or that we're the ones who chose to go to sleep): When we close ourselves to love, we often forget that we were the ones who chose to close ourselves to it.

We build barriers and walls. We forget love exists as a possibility for us altogether.

And if we do that for too long, we lose awareness of the golden thread.

I don't want you to ever forget the golden thread is there.

Because when people forget that, suffering gets magnified, not happiness.

Hurt people hurt people. Scared people do scary things.

That's not a guilt trip, it's simply how darkness spreads.

And yes, that's part of the process too. But not the part this book aims to play.

I don't want to condemn your darkness should you find yourself in it.

I just want to offer a golden thread that can help guide your way home.

Maybe it will, maybe it won't. But I'm trusting that whatever I write today is exactly what wants to be written. And whatever you're reading today is exactly what you want to read.

Sure, there's a part of me that's scared of these words making some impact I didn't intend, but that's not up to me to decide.

We can never be certain that people will recognize the love within our words and actions.

All we can do is keep riding our wave and trust it.

The only thing we can be certain of in life is physical death.

I think it's no coincidence that so many people find clarity, love and forgiveness on their deathbed. Or see their lives flashing in front of their eyes.

It seems to me like that's what it would look like for the wave to collapse back into the whole. Every event, person and feeling we ever got to experience, finally having walked us home.

CHAPTER 21
GIVING YOUR POWER AWAY

Freedom isn't just how many resources, options or actions we have available to us.

It's also about how many different experiences we allow ourselves to have while still staying in touch with our power.

And how many options we see as valid or available to us in any given situation.

How many different flavors of love can you allow yourself to feel without losing awareness of your undercurrent of happiness?

How many ways of being —or types of behavior— can you allow yourself to engage in without condemning or judging yourself for it?

To which degree do you allow yourself to feel at choice — even when on paper it seems like you have none?

Ten years ago I felt extremely unhappy with my life.

I felt hopeless, frustrated and miserable, and I had felt that way since forever.

Until I read this one sentence and it changed everything:

"Which is more likely:

That for you to be happy, everyone and everything else has to change?

Or that for you to be happy you have to change?"

There's only one helpful answer. Because let's be honest:

If you're not feeling happy right now, what are you going to do?

Change an entire society?

Change every single person you'll ever date?

Re-write the entire last season of Game of Thrones and go film it yourself?

That sort of thinking is only going to keep you stuck.

And this is not about who's to blame for how you feel.

It's about getting unstuck and opening up to new possibilities.

People are boring? Become more interested.

Friends mistreat you? Find different ones.

Hate doing laundry? Stop wearing clothes.

Ask yourself *"How am I contributing to the continuation of these conditions that I dislike? And what am I gonna do about it?"*

What can you change about the way you think or act or interpret things that will make things better for you?

When I share this perspective with people, they often feel triggered or offended.

Which is understandable..

I'm sure that had this phrase reached me at a different time in my life, I would've reacted with anger myself.

The reason for that (in my case, which might differ from other people's), is that I was operating from a paradigm of shame, blame and victimhood.

For example, here's how I likely would have responded to someone sharing with me the phrase I just shared with you:

"Are you seriously saying that I'm the one who has to change?

That the problem is me rather than the fact that we live in a messed up society where the majority of people are insane?

That's just blaming the victim for everyone else's behavior!"

I have a lot of compassion for the version of me who would have said that.

And also, if I could give him anything, I'd give him his freedom and power back.

So to my younger self, or anyone feeling that way about it, I'd like to emphasize:

You are not the problem.

You are not to blame.

But you *are* the one responsible.

Responsibility and blame are two very different things.

And when you confuse their meanings, you disempower yourself.

Blame is an illusory paradigm in which we believe that if somehow the right person would get punished for the mess we're in, it would alleviate our pain and we'd finally be able to accept things and find peace.

But the truth is:

1. No matter how many people we punish, we can't create a utopia in which humans will stop perpetrating against each other.

2. We will accept things when we're ready and willing to do so.

3. We'll find peace when we're ready and willing to find it.

Yes, finding peace may coincide with the moment someone is held accountable for our misery.

But if they do coincide, the reason is usually still that it was our own decision to be at peace.

After all, it was us who declared *"Once this person is held accountable, I'll finally be at peace"*.

That's a decision.

A clear decision to postpone peace and acceptance.

And give our power away to some external person or event.

Blame is an illusion, but responsibility is not.

So if someone says you are responsible, they're not saying you're to blame.

They are not placing the burden of blame on you. They are giving you a way to finally lift that burden.

To blame is to BE-LAME. To be responsible is to be RESPONSE-ABLE.

Isn't that a beautiful miracle?

To go from injured and powerless ("lame") to being "ABLE" to respond again?

Simply by changing a word in your thoughts?

This is how to increase your personal power and claim your freedom back:

Find all the areas, experiences or feelings in life where you are placing responsibility on outside circumstances and choose to take responsibility yourself.

Even if others helped create the mess you're in (or created most of it), blaming them can't make them take more responsibility. But it **will** disempower **you.**

There is no way to force another person to take responsibility for anything.

So there's no point in trying to figure out who's responsible for how much of a situation and what they should do about it. All you can do is:

A). Take up responsibility yourself

B). Leave it to others but accept that it was you who left it to them (in which case you use your power to delegate, but you don't lose the power)

That doesn't mean there aren't aspects of society that need change.

That doesn't mean real perpetrators shouldn't be held accountable for their actions.

All it means is that letting your happiness and success depend on those things is denying yourself the very happiness you seek.

You can't change what happened to you.

But you can change how you relate to it.

It might seem like it *deserves* to be related to in a certain way.

But ask yourself: Who is impacted by the way you relate to it?

Mostly you. Not the event.

Because the event has long passed.

Now all that's left is how you relate to it.

In 2016, I tried to write a book about freedom.

Each chapter discussed a common impediment to personal freedom, followed by advice on how to liberate yourself from it.

Topics ranged from chronic fear and shame to social conditioning, escaping the 9 to 5 or dealing with what I saw as "culturally enforced monogamy".

Halfway through writing it, I became aware of the ridiculousness of my own pursuit.

I spent years identifying what I wanted to be free from and how to free myself of it.

But the irony is, the very fact that I was trying to do so is what was preventing me from being free. The harder you try to be free from a limitation, the more the perceived limitation holds you in its grasp.

When you fight something, you help it grow stronger. You are giving it more and more control over you. Each time you mention the thing you're trying to be free from, you are re-affirming its power.

For example:

If you're trying to be free from social conditioning by breaking norms for the sake of it, you are emphasizing them.

Each time a normbreak gets accepted, you'll find a new norm that is not accepted yet. Thereby re-creating the experience of still not being free.

On top of that, you are putting out an invitational energy for people to judge you. Because that's what your rebellion sets out to prove.

Imagine there was no one out there to cast any judgment.

That every possible behavior was accepted as long as it didn't cause harm.

What would you do then?

Would you still be doing all the same things you're now doing in an attempt to break norms?

Doing something with the purpose to break a norm is not liberation.

It's letting your actions be dictated *by* that very norm.

You are still following it, you're just following it in reverse.

To be truly free, you have to let go of the idea altogether.

Rather than focusing on fighting against perceived prison guards by pushing the boundaries, ask yourself:

In your heart of hearts, if you didn't know what other people were doing or saying, what would *you* want to do?

The answer might break a norm or not. That is irrelevant.

If it happens to stand out from the crowd, great. If it blends in and follows the norms, equally great. Doesn't matter. Don't pay attention to it.

As long as it doesn't intend to harm anyone, just do the thing.

You don't have to struggle, fight, work on, or change to be *"free from"* something, because you always have been *free to*.

This is the realization that ended my book at the time:

You don't need to be *"free from"* anything anymore once you realize you're already *"free to"*.

Instead of trying to be *"free from"* the emotional pain caused by someone who hurt you in the past, how about realizing you're *"free to"* bring joy, nourishment and relaxation to this moment, right now?

Instead of trying to be *"free from"* your insecurities, how about realizing you're already *"free to"* act in spite of them, even if it feels uncomfortable at first?

Instead of trying to be *"free from"* a job you're getting tired of, how about realizing you are *"free to"* quit and walk out if you want to?

—*But won't quitting my job leave me without money then?* —

Possibly. And that might be a good reason to stay.

But remember: it's still your choice.

You have the freedom to choose the unpleasant elements of one reality (keeping your job) over those of another (financial stress).

Freedom isn't the disappearance of limitations. There will always be limitations.

Freedom is the power to act, speak or think as you want.

And as long as you accept responsibility for the outcome of that, those can not be taken from you in any way.

People might enforce serious repercussions on you for choosing a certain option.

Repercussions large enough to make it a logical choice to choose the option they want you to.

But you're still at choice.

The option of choosing to accept whatever threat they're trying to coerce you with, still exists an option. Doesn't make it a smart option. But it's an option nonetheless.

They can't *actually* control you.

Only provide compelling incentives.

Dropping your victim identity does not mean denying you were victimized.

The attitude of victimhood is separate from the event of being victimized.

Sometimes they occur together, sometimes it's one without the other.

Victim empowerment is not the same as victim blaming.

What does it mean to give your power away?

You give your power away every time you believe you need permission or assistance from an outside source to take decisions or actions.

Many people would read the above phrase and say *"No shit, Sherlock"*.

(Other people name themselves "Snoop" and say *"No shizzle, Shernizzle"* instead. Whatever floats your boat!)

But as simple as it sounds, let me assure you:

I've never met a person who doesn't give their power away in at least one area of their lives.

It goes a lot deeper than you'd expect.

(That's what she said).

For example, many people give their power away when it comes to having permission to feel loved:

- They may think they need to be in perfect shape to receive love.

- They may think they need more money or fancy clothes to receive love.

- Some even think it depends on the fortune of meeting the right person.

In all cases, you are giving away your power to something outside you, which blocks the possibility of you following your authentic desires.

There are many reasons we give our power away. But the main essence is this:

We fear the responsibility that comes with our power.

We do this because we either fear blame (which we confuse with responsibility) or fear the perceived burden of responsibility itself.

Fearing the burden of responsibility looks like this:

Let's say you want to get in great shape.

Whatever getting in great shape looks like to you, you have the power to do this:

- Keep track of what you eat.
- If you want to lose weight, eat less calories than you burn.
- If you want to gain weight, eat more.
- Find a training program that suits your needs and follow it.

But doing this consistently is a responsibility many people don't want to take on.

Enter the helpful concept of giving your power away:

- Giving it away to finding the right fat loss supplement.
- Giving it away to "needing" a personal trainer but not having the money.
- Giving it away by trying to follow the restrictive rules of some fad diet and then failing.
- Giving it away to saying *"I don't have enough discipline"* but not Googling how to be more consistent with habits.

It's very convenient to give your power away to such things.

Because if you don't succeed, you can ignore the fact that you didn't do the work and say:

- *"The supplement didn't work. I'll find a better one."*
- *"New research shows there's another diet that's better than the previous twelve I tried."*

Or the classic:

- *"I guess I just have bad genetics" (while never counting calories consistently).*

But here's the truth:

You are the only person with the power to get yourself in shape.

You are responsible for taking the required actions.

So the question is simple:

What will you do with your power?

Do you choose to be in shape? Or do you choose not to have to do all the work?

Both choices are perfectly fine to make.

The idea of wanting the perfect body may in itself be something that came for giving your power away.

(For example: By thinking you need a certain body shape to feel happy or attractive.)

The point is again, unless the reason is *"because I genuinely want to"* there's no real reason why you need a six pack.

Not even a four pack. Or a 2pac.

And as we've seen before: *"I want to"* only means you want to when it means *"I want all of it"*, not "I want some parts of it".

Giving our power away is often a form of not being honest with ourselves.

When we reclaim our power, we're free to say:

"You know what, I don't really want this thing. So I'll seize my efforts." or *"I do want this thing, so I'll take the responsible actions required to make it happen."*

Without the unnecessary suffering of telling ourselves we want something, then holding a bunch of random stuff responsible for not getting it and feeling frustrated because of that.

It's lunacy.

But it's a popular lunacy.

Giving away our power because we confuse responsibility with blame looks like this:

Imagine you are put on a project or task at work. And you're the one responsible for its completion.

What usually matters in these cases is that a specific outcome is achieved.

Still, many people will ask for step by step instructions on how to complete the project instead.

Why?

Because when we give our power away to the person who gave the instructions, nobody can blame us.

If the next day the boss comes around and asks *"Who did this job so badly?"*, you can say *"I was just following orders, Madam."* and deflect all blame.

But in reality you always had the choice to defy the orders.

No orders or instructions can take away your power.

One of the reasons I suspect that we don't often hear about taking radical responsibility for our experience is this:

People who give their power away are a terrific source of income.

If instead of this book — which tells you that who you are right now is just fine — I'd write a book about how *"personal transformation rarely ever happens without the guidance of a good coach"*, I could then benefit from you having that belief.

You see, if I am a coach, then as long as I can make people believe that *I* have the power, not them, they are more likely to consider hiring me to "fix their problems".

This is the business model behind a shocking amount of consumer goods and services.

If we knew that we could fix our sleep by changing your habits, would we still need sleeping pills?

If we knew that our own pheromones smelled sexy, would we still need to buy expensive perfume to believe we smell attractive?

The answer is no.

But of course, you might still buy it because you want to. Because you like the smell for its own sake.

I'm giving this example, to illustrate the importance of being free "to". Not free "from".

You don't have to be free "from" perfume.

Because when that's what you believe, suddenly you don't have the option of wearing perfume anymore!

It's when you become "free to" that you are truly free.

Some days you may want to wear it. Other days not. It will make no difference to how you feel about yourself.

When you take radical responsibility, you are free to do what you want.

You can have organic food. You can have non-organic food. You can dumpster dive if that's what you want.

You don't complain when one of those options is not available.

You are merely making choices and accepting their consequences. Without limiting yourself.

That's how freedom starts.

With you recognizing your own power and responsibility.

Have you ever done something because you were told to, even when you didn't really believe it was right?

How about seeing someone do something wrong and feeling bad about it but not speaking up because you thought "it's not my responsibility to call them out"?

Those are common ways in which people give their power away.

And this has contributed to some of the most horrifying things ever happening to humans.

Hitler, Mao, Pol Pot, and many many more...could these have succeeded in slaughtering so many people if nobody gave their power away?

Of course not.

It is unthinkable that Hitler himself would have single handedly killed so many people without being stopped.

Or that one dictator would be able to bend a whole country to their will.

Each of them needed other people who gave their power away to achieve it.

And a lot of people willingly handed it over because they didn't know they had it.

A common narrative about this is that people got misinformed, manipulated or persuaded by evil leaders.

And there is truth to that. Human minds can be influenced.

But we can only be influenced by things we give our power away to .

If you give your powers of discerning truth away to an ideology, an expert in a lab coat, the media or "peer pressure", then yes, you can be manipulated by all of those.

But as any good hypnotist knows, a person who doesn't want to be hypnotized is extremely hard to hypnotize.

Because all hypnosis is actually self-hypnosis.

The reason hypnotists can hypnotize you is because you are giving your power away to them.

So the idea that Hitler was just this massively powerful pencil mustache that swayed an entire country against their will is only part of the story.

Every single person that helped them carry out this vision, was someone who gave their power away.

By which I'm not saying they're to blame for what happened.

Remember: Responsibility and blame are different things.

I imagine that many didn't even know they were giving their power away(After all, when have you last heard anyone talk about this concept?)

I also imagine that many others kept their power but chose the safest option available to them.

So the question arises: Can't circumstances *force* you to give your power away?

What if the choice is something like *"follow these terrible orders or be sent to the torture camps"*?

Indeed, there are many factors that might lead someone to engage in behavior they normally wouldn't support:

- Believing their judgment to be inferior to that of a person in an authoritative role
- The (very valid) fear of retaliation and the consequence of not complying
- Wanting to avoid confrontation
- (Extreme) Social pressure
- Threats

And there are many reasons why people at large scale might defer their power to a dangerous leader, even when not under coercion:

- Economic conditions
- Political instability
- Societal issues

We shouldn't judge someone for complying when faced with such forces.

Many of us would act the same way being in such a situation.

And you and I can't know if we would, until we find ourselves in the middle of it.

Which I hope never happens.

But know this:

If you were coerced into doing something that went against your own integrity, you did not lose your power.

And you didn't become a bad person either.

You used your power to make a decision that was in integrity with your predicament at that moment.

You are not to blame. Even though you remained response-able.

Because here's the thing: It's impossible to give your power away.

Nobody has the power to make you do anything unless you decide to temporarily hand them your power.

Every decision you make is still yours.

You don't have to follow every decision your boss makes.

They're just a person *you* are outsourcing your decision to by putting them in that role.

You are still the one making the choice that guides your actions.

Even if you follow orders or *"just do what everyone around you does"*, you are making the choice to do so.

You also have the option to disagree and do something different.

That doesn't mean you should never use your power to follow someone's orders, or to do as everyone else.

We *need* group coherence. We *need* people in leadership roles to coordinate complex projects.

Sometimes we *need* for people to unite behind a singular idea so that it can become a reality.

Because our survival depends on each other.

But choosing to follow someone's lead does not take the power away from you.

Every step of the way, decide over and over again whether you agree with what you are participating in or not.

I believe that when people stop giving their power away to a story told by a leader or ideology, very few would honestly answer *"Yes, I want to go and commit a genocide today"*.

Think of a dictatorship:

If everyone in the army would simultaneously tell their superiors *"I refuse to harm our citizens"* and if all their superiors did the same, all the way up the chain, no citizens would be harmed.

The dictator only has power because of the large number of people giving *their* power away.

And many of them might have a good reason to do so. Their survival might depend on it.

So again, let's not cast blame.

In fact, I must admit, because of how tough it can be for people to internalize the distinction between responsibility and blame, I'm scared of including this chapter in the book.

I'm scared because my intention is to give a gift of love, not of guilt.

I do not wish to impact people in ways that promote guilt or blame.

But I believe this message can also save lives, so I'm taking the risk.

Because not everyone who contributes to committing atrocities might do so out of survival necessity.

I believe that for many people, it happens because they're not aware of their own power.

And I want you to know that whatever is happening to you, or whatever happened to you in the past:

You have your power. It can not be taken from you.

That doesn't mean you are under any obligation to defy orders or to act against your own survival needs.

All I want is for you to know you'll always have it.

No matter what happens.

No matter how disempowering things can feel.

You are free, you are powerful, and you can rise above.

We don't just have to be careful with giving our power away to ideologies commonly agreed upon as bad (like nazism) but also to popular positive causes like climate activism or inclusivity.

I once met a person who wanted to save the world from sexism.

She believed that being extremely sexist against men would achieve that (because it would "restore the balance").

I doubt that if she hadn't given her power away to an extremist ideology, she would've said *"Yes, I believe that spreading the exact thing I hate will result in creating less of it."*

Whomever you choose to side with. No matter which positive cause or holy book guides your choices, always remember:

No one else is responsible for the choices you make or the beliefs you hold.

This is true even in extreme situations.

If someone held a gun to my head and said *"I'll shoot you unless you punch an innocent puppy to death."*

Would they have forced me to kill a puppy?

No, they wouldn't.

In this hypothetical scenario, I still kept my power.

I could choose the option of dying (or doing nothing and hoping they don't shoot).

I could choose to risk my life trying to take the gun from them (and let's be honest, I'd probably fail).

And sadly, it's quite possible that I'd choose to kill the puppy and then feel horrified about what I'd done.

Would you have killed the puppy?

And if so, would that make you evil?

Of course not.

Nobody would blame you for choosing not to die.

Even if you love puppies, staying alive allows you to start a charity that saves many more puppies afterwards if you want to.

I hope you never have to make a decision about punching puppies to death. But again, in the unlikely event that it happens:

You did not lose your power.

The gun wouldn't have made you kill that puppy.

The gun would've just presented you with a very difficult decision (or an easy one, depending on how you look at it).

The decision was still yours.

And that is OK.

It doesn't make you to blame because blame doesn't exist.

It doesn't make you bad because you acted out of self-love.

I'm repeating this, because from the illusory paradigm of blame, the things I'm saying here would be considered highly offensive.

But I'm using this extreme topic to make a point:

That nobody can ever take your freedom.

And if they tried to, it might very well feel like they succeeded in doing so, because the freedom might be buried under a lot of pain and trauma that still needs to be felt.

But that doesn't mean it's gone.

Power can be hard to claim back when it's been abused.

But just like love, your power and freedom are always there, waiting to be found by you.

Cheering you on in your search.

Keeping a bottle of champagne ready in the fridge, to celebrate once you reclaim them.

Of course, we have to acknowledge the elephant in the room:

As free and powerful as you are, some limitations are very, very real.

If you have only one leg, you have less options for physical movement than people with two legs.

And if you're broke, you have less options for spending money than people who are wealthy.

That said, in all cases, you have equal freedom to choose what you do with the options available to you.

This is the difference between the player (you) and the state of the gameworld (what's happening).

It's impossible for a gameworld not to have limitations.

Without limitations, a thing can not exist.

The only thing that has no limitations, is infinity. The ocean of existence itself.

Anything that can be pointed out as existing separately requires at least one limitation to exist.

And that's the limitation of its opposite.

Light can't exist without the limitation of not being dark.

In order for you to be alive, you already have to limit yourself.

Because you can only be alive as long as you don't die.

All the rules and limitations in the gameworld "life" exist because the limitation of death exists.

If death didn't exist, why eat? Why work? Why wear a seatbelt?

Why treasure any experience? You could have it a million times over till infinity.

Similarly, the gameworld of handball couldn't exist if you were allowed to use your feet in it.

Without that limitation, it would just be a game of ball.

Every day you are participating in hundreds of games without knowing.

As we walk through the world, you and I are always moving from gameworld to gameworld. (and usually we're in multiple of those at once).

Each gameworld has its own rules, which players follow.

And we follow them so well that they feel like second nature to us.

For example:

You can wear a bikini on most western beaches (in fact, on many of them you don't even need to wear one). But if you'd wear a bikini to work, suddenly your co-workers would all stare at you.

That's because "beach" is a different gameworld than "office".

In theory, it wouldn't matter if you went swimming in a three piece suit, or gave a presentation in a bra and panties. But we've all agreed that those are not things we do in those gameworlds.

So we stick to it.

It's important to realize that none of these gameworlds really exist.

Only the ocean of existence itself exists.

But because we all pretend the gameworlds are real, we are subject to their limitations.

When playing the game of supermarket, you queue in a nice line and await your turn at the cash register.

But when you play the game of nightclub, you clamor for attention from the barman, try to make eye contact and hope they pick you soon (it probably helps if you wear a suit or a bikini).

If you try swapping the two approaches, it doesn't work very well.

The people in the supermarket will be angry at you. And the people in the nightclub will ignore you.

Society in itself is a gameworld which contains infinite sub-games, minigames and side quests.

Money for example, is a sub-game most people have agreed to join.

To play it, you have to pretend random pieces of paper —or digits on a screen— hold value.

Then you have to find a way to obtain them by interacting with other players of the money game.

You might give those players some of your time.

You could solve a problem for them or publish a weird book like this one.

However, if you'd try to do this with someone who doesn't play the money game, they'd be quite confused when after helping them out with something, you ask for a stack of papers with portraits of dead presidents on them.

Especially if they're not playing the president game either.

But why am I telling you all this?

Understanding gameworlds will have a huge impact on your freedom.

Firstly, because if you want to get anywhere in any game, you have to know you're in it.

Wherever you are. If there are humans, there's a game being played.

If you don't know what the game is, you don't know its limitations. But you might still be subject to them. And that can keep you stuck.

Secondly, if you don't know you're in a gameworld, you can confuse it with reality. And this can make reality very frustrating and absurd.

Imagine for a moment that you're a dog (might be easier to do for some readers than others).

Being the dog that you are, one thing you really love doing is jumping on your human's lap after a long day of exhausting doggery.

Your human loves to watch Netflix in their sweatpants and they're always happy to cuddle with you on the couch.

But one day, your human comes home in a suit (because they went to play the office game).

You jump on their lap as usual, but they scold you and push you away.

You try jumping again.

Now they yell "BAD DOG!" and slap you on the nose.

What did you learn (besides potentially discovering a few new turnons)?

You might think *"I learned I shouldn't jump on my human when they're wearing a suit"*.

But you'd be wrong.

Because being a dog, you don't know about the rules of the suit game.

Dogs live in reality. Where clothing is a means to keep yourself warm, and nothing else.

Only humans live in the matrix where suits and sweatpants somehow mean different things.

So all you know is:

"Normally my human loves it when I jump on him.

But on random moments, they react by scolding me instead.

It's confusing and it makes me sad.

Sincerely,

Dog."

This is what happens when you're unaware of your current gameworld.

And it is a surprisingly common experience for humans to have (because of Rule #0, but we'll get to that later).

Lastly, knowing which gameworld you are in is essential for inter-gameworld communication.

If you're assuming we're playing one game, while the other person's playing another, it can lead to a breakdown in understanding.

For instance, when you're playing *"let's take the bus"* in Tokyo, one of the rules is that the bus is always on time.

But when you're playing *"let's take the bus"* in some parts of Lagos, you might find there isn't even a time listed. And if there was, you'd be wiser not to plan your day based on it.

So if you'd complain to the bus driver about being late in Lagos, you're confusing the gameworld and coming across as a dufus.

I once landed in a foreign country and from the second I got off the plane, I was getting ambushed by people trying to sell me stuff.

(Literally, the airport security tried to sell me a football team before I even passed passport control.)

I assumed they just saw me as a dollar sign. But that wasn't the full story:

To me, if a purchase is not functional, spreading joy or fulfilling a need, I see no reason to buy it.

I know this can be frustrating for sales people (and in this case, it seemed all people were sales people).

Each new day I was met with increasing antagonism from locals.

The more I didn't buy their stuff, the more angry and aggressive they got.

I tried to fix it with kind words like:

"I wish you well. But I simply don't need what you're offering to me."

It was friendlier than saying *"piss off!"* but I still missed the point.

One day, a woman tried to sell me bananas.

I didn't want bananas. But she pleaded with me, saying *"Sir, I need money for food."*

I tried to offer her one of the bananas. She refused.

At some point, a local friend told me : *"The rest of the village is angry at you because you reject their friendship."*

I thought *"What? I'm friendly to everyone. They are the ones who disrespect my boundaries."*

Here's what I learned had happened:

From my perspective, buying stuff is a neutral exchange of value.

You have what I want. I have what you want. Let's trade.

From the perspective of the locals, an exchange of goods was the initiation of a friendship.

Me not spending $1 on something I didn't need meant I was telling them *"I enter your village but refuse to come as a friend."*

I was in a foreign gameworld, acting as if I was still in the one from my hometown.

If nobody had told me how their gameworld worked, I might have believed I was simply *"surrounded by desperate and pushy sales people"*.

Knowing the gameworld, I was free to choose if I wanted to play by its rules or not.

Which brings us to rule 0.

Each gameworld you join is defined by the following parameters:

- A context (we follow the rules of the game when we're in the context, but stop doing so when the context changes)
- An intended outcome (what's to be achieved by playing)
- Rules of engagement (how to play the game)
- Rule #0

Now you might be wondering, "what's rule 0?"

Rule 0 is the reason you don't know you're in a gameworld.

Rule 0 dictates:

"As long as we're playing this game, we will continue to pretend it's not a game."

One of the best ways to see rule 0 in action, is to watch people who hate each other play the game of politeness together.

Rule 0 is essential because without it, the game wouldn't work.

When you're playing monopoly for example, you'll never hear a player say *"Dang, I'm running out of monopoly money here..."*

No, for the duration of the game, they'll pretend the money is real.

Without rule 0, running out of monopoly money might lead to people saying *"whatever, I'll have a beer instead"*.

But rule 0 motivates your mind to stay in the game, come up with solutions and get back on top.

When someone cheats or flips the table, suddenly we become aware of rule 0 again and say *"Relax buddy, we're just playing!"*

The same is true about every gameworld in life.

Whether it's business, relationships, or hanging the toilet roll in a particular direction.

The moment someone cheats, you're reminded that there's a game with rules. And that they broke one.

(Yes, rule 0 is another example of love playing hide and seek ;-))

However, it's important to remember that the limitations of the gameworld are not the limitations of reality.

They apply for as long as you want to stay in the game.

The people who are still subject to rule 0 will tell you *"you can't do that"*.

But I assure you, it's very much physically possible to put pineapple on pizza.

We play games with limitations because limitations and challenges make things interesting.

There are certain experiences you simply can't have without creating limitations.

How much fun is it to challenge yourself to hop on one leg? Or wear a blindfold?

Life is obviously better when you have all your limbs and eyes.

But occasionally, we want to experience limitations.

Because they stimulate creativity and make us more aware of the possibilities and freedom we still have in such a situation.

Limitlessness and infinity might be blissful but they're also monotonous.

Imagine you were no longer a wave. Only the ocean.

No longer human but an omnipotent power.

You could do anything you ever wanted.

But you were also infinite, which would mean you're already doing every infinite thing that could possibly exist. All at the same time. Forever.

In that case, there still be one thing missing from your infinite list of superpowers:

The ability to be powerless.

And there'd be one thing missing from your infinite existence:

Limitations.

The only way to experience those (and finally have everything) would be to hide your own power and freedom from yourself.

Sounds familiar by now? I bet it does.

Why did we do this whole exploration of the concept of "gameworlds"?

To make a distinction between real limitations on *your* freedom and the limitations you believe you have because of the gameworlds you're in.

You always have your freedom.

You always have the power to make a choice about what you do in response to anything that happens.

But if you want to stay in the gameworld you're currently in, you have to accept its limitations and the hand you're dealt.

Sometimes your hypothetical choices are *"punch a puppy to death or leave the game of life"*.

And because of rule 0, we can't know if life is just another gameworld (with something "outside of it") or if it is the ultimate reality.

So we will do anything we can to be able to continue playing it.

Depending on the hand you were dealt, the game of life can be very harsh.

Like being born in poverty, growing up without parents or having your country ravaged by war.

I do not wish such reality upon anyone. Nor do I wish to make light of it.

But I do want to make the distinction that the limitations of the situation you find yourself in, do not take away your inherent power or freedom to make choices *within* that situation.

There are people like Nelson Mandela, Viktor Frankl or Malala Yousafzai who found themselves in situations where so many freedoms were removed by their gameworlds, that it feels heretical to even use the term "gameworld" to describe them.

Yet these people somehow managed to continue to see through the illusion of powerlessness.

To see that no matter how badly their environment treated them. No matter how many times they had absolutely no choice in their external response, no one could ever take away their power or freedom to choose their *internal* response.

They show us that no matter how badly the cards are stacked against us, nobody can take away our ability to choose how we play them.

Even if that means that for a long time, you have to do exactly what people want you to do, just to stay in the game of life.

Full freedom includes the freedom to be constrained, too.

Without that, we're just constraining ourselves to only accepting experiences in which we're not constrained, which is a logical impossibility.

(And with that said: May you experience as little constraints as possible in this life.

Or perhaps just the right amount to minimize your suffering and maximize your meaning.)

I used to create this story in my head that I deserved better than the circumstances I was given.

That I should've been dealt better cards in life.

But here's the truth: Nobody deserves anything.

You don't "deserve" better than what you have.

And "bad people" don't "deserve" to have it any worse or to be punished.

Don't get me wrong though.

It's not that you aren't worthy of deserving.

— If you'd ask me, I'd say you deserve nothing less than all the love in the world.—

It's also not that evil shouldn't be held accountable.

No, this all has nothing to do with you or me, or other people's actions.

Nobody deserves anything, because "deserving" isn't real.

All you have to do to expose the illusion of "deserving" is sit down and try to "deserve" something.

You can't. It's not physically possible.

It's a fantasy arising from entitlement or blame (which as we know, are both fantasies too).

No amount of "deserving" can change things.

How can you change things? By reclaiming your own power, freedom and responsibility. And accepting the limitations you are faced with.

Remember: To go anywhere, you have to start where you are. To change anything, you have to first accept it.

There's another downside to focusing too much on the bad cards you were dealt.

It stops you from seeing all the good ones.

By focusing on the cards in life I didn't like —such as abuse, loneliness, or living in a system that didn't seem to be made for me— I failed to notice all the great cards that were in my hand too.

Like being born middle class in a country with a good economy. Or the fact that my parents loved me, while so many others grew up in challenging households.

I could spend my life complaining about all the ways I was harmed and violated as a kid.

And all of my complaints would be valid. But by focusing on them, I'd be denying all the privileges I received which many others did not. And I'd be denying all that I was spared from, which many others were not.

The way I see it now:

We all have ways in which we're disadvantaged (and these are always unequal, because otherwise they would not be disadvantages).

We also all have ways in which we are *advantaged*. Even if we can't see it.

I can't speak for anyone else, because I've never experienced anyone else's disadvantages directly. But accepting my own was a crucial step to finding my power back.

And it taught me that denying or downplaying my privileges also meant denying myself what I was given and denying the world of any ways I could use them to serve others.

I'm not saying "ignore the negative and focus only on the positive". Because our disadvantages are very real.

But I invite you to start welcoming both as aspects of the experience we're having in this life.

What good is the wealth you were born into if you don't want to use it because you are ashamed of that privilege?

What good is the love one parent gave you if you stay focused on the fact that the other didn't?

When we demonize our privileges, we let them go to waste.

When we deny our limitations, they become invisible roadblocks.

We're always limited in some ways and we're always privileged in others.

Unfortunately, this balance is nowhere near equal. Not everyone's disadvantages are balanced by their privileges.

Some people may face systemic oppression, trauma, or marginalization that overwhelms their opportunities or advantages.

I can't tell you how to play your hand, because the only experience I have is playing my own.

And if the one you're dealt was worse than mine, I'm not going to claim you should be happy about that.

But I do believe there are some things we can all benefit from, no matter what we start out with:

- To accept the limitations we're faced with (which doesn't mean to be complacent about them).
- To not reject our privileges but wear them with humility and grace.
- To forgive ourselves and others when we inevitably fail to do so (because we're all human).
- Perhaps at some point, to forgive the world we're in for the imbalances and limitations that exist on a larger scale.

(All of course, without forcing ourselves to do any of these: Because the capacity we're given in each moment to do so is simply another limitation to accept.)

It's not that you are not free because of the limitations placed upon you.

It's that you are free *and* limitations were placed upon you.

The idea that we are free even when faced with limitations and that a large part of our suffering is created by refusing to see how much freedom and power we have is offensive to many.

Because accepting our inner freedom and power can trigger grief over all the self-induced suffering we've endured on top of any initial harm that was done to us by others.

This grief can include blaming ourselves for perpetuating the suffering which creates an even stronger need for forgiveness.

Forgiving ourselves and others is a doorway to a reality that feels oddly different than it looks like from the outside.

So different that explaining it can sound like horse poop to someone who hasn't experienced it.

It is no exaggeration that forgiveness is a gift as much to the forgiver as to the forgivee.

Forgiveness is the exact moment when love finally finds itself again inside your heart after an exceptionally tough game of hide and seek.

The harder it was to forgive, the more triumphant love's return.

And when it returns, it comes bearing the gifts of freedom, responsibility and power.

Freedom, because you are now no longer bound by carrying around resentment.

Responsibility because that's what freedom really is deep down: The ability to choose your response.

It's when we feel we are not free or don't have power that we can't choose our response.

Which happens to be exactly when most people's behavior becomes "irresponsible".

In fact, many perpetrators strongly believe they are victims.

They act blindly and irresponsibly because they feel powerless.

One of the most common ways in which we use our innate power is to hide it. To appear inconspicuous.

Because what's more powerful than power? Invisible power!

But make no mistake:

Just as with love, the fact that your power is hiding doesn't mean you don't have it.

You always have it, whether you believe so or not.

Forgive more.

Not to let people off the hook, but to break the cycle.

The history of the world (and the family) is filled with horrors perpetrated by people who felt justified by their own victimization.

Forgiveness is healing.

The tricky part of underestimating your own power is that you may be impacting others in ways you don't see.

For example, in my early teens, I was a pushover in many ways.

I would let others cross my boundaries, or if they'd ask me something, I'd say "yes" by default.

Luckily, I wasn't surrounded by people who would bully me.

But at the same time, if they wanted something from me, they'd get it. Because I lacked the dignity to deny their requests.

As I grew more confident, I started to embrace my authentic voice and desires. I felt completely free to do whatever felt true to me.

During this period, I considered freedom my #1 value in life.

Which worked great for me. But not always for everyone else.

For example, I would crash other people's party's on a daily basis, and act as if their place was my private playground.

I was unknowingly crossing other people's boundaries in the exact same way mine used to be crossed. I didn't see how my behavior could be harmful for others.

I wasn't aware that just myself a few years before, a lot of them lacked the self-empowerment to stand up to me if my behavior wasn't something they agreed with.

(How could I not see that? Because I was still so obsessed with my own victim stories that it didn't occur to me that other people could have similar challenges.)

I didn't realize that I had power. I didn't realize that my freedom was a form of power.

One day a good friend told me *"When freedom is your only value, you create an imbalance in your personality. You become a steamroller, rolling over everyone else's freedom, while celebrating your right to yours."*.

We pondered what values might balance out my personality, and settled on "Love".

Freedom without love can easily turn into oppression.

The very thing it believes it is free from.

The more you re-claim your freedom and power, the more you might be in situations where it's easy to take space from others without knowing so.

Not necessarily in a way that crosses boundaries.

But as a byproduct of that fact, if you're the most socially free person in a room, it becomes easy to unknowingly dominate every interaction with your presence.

Not everyone is always aware of their power and freedom.

So the more you become aware of it, the more important it becomes to use it wisely, humbly and kindly.

Remember what it felt like to be stuck in the hardest game of hide and seek you got to play so far.

Remember how good it felt when you finally found the love, freedom, power and responsibility inside yourself.

Then ask yourself what you want for others: That they all get to find themselves?

Or for them to experience the illusion of not having power in response to you using yours?

You are free to do with your newfound power as you please.

Yet my hope is that you use it to do the most good possible.

And that whenever you or I end up using it in questionable ways (we will), we catch ourselves quickly, forgive ourselves easily, and find our way home to love.

CHAPTER 22
I COMMAND YOU TO LEAD ME

"Anxiety is the dizziness of freedom."

— Soren Kierkegaard

One reason we give our own power away and deny ourselves our freedom is we don't believe we can handle it.

When faced with the boundlessness of our own possibilities... what are we supposed to do?

How do we choose from among the endless possibilities at our disposal?

And what if we choose the wrong thing?

It's popular to claim we want freedom, but how many of us really want the reality of it?

Because when we have it, we sure seem to go to great lengths to forget we do.

As a kid, you deferred to your parents for most major decisions.

Later, that role was taken up by teachers, mentors or managers.

And there were times when you wished they'd just let you do your thing rather than boss you around.

But for a large majority of people, when they are truly allowed to do their thing without any imposed structure or limitations, they get anxious.

"What if I ruin it all? What if stepping into my own power and authority is what messes up my life? Could I ever forgive myself for that? Could I deal with the consequences?"

Most humans have a persistent subconscious desire for someone to tell them exactly how to live their lives.

In the past, religion and institutionalized philosophies provided unquestionable answers to unanswerable questions.

Or the answers were already there at birth, because people were born into a situation where there was only one path laid out for them: The path of their local culture, which they couldn't step out of.

But in many modern societies, you get to choose your job, your life philosophy *and* your religion.

Which is a great freedom, but it also comes with the accompanying dizziness.

Because now that those things aren't enforced on you, they can no longer inform your choices without being questioned.

Where in the past, you might have accepted the decrees of your religion or culture blindly, now you may wonder *"Do I believe the right things?"*.

In other words: Religion is no longer deciding for you which rules to follow. You are deciding which religion you follow.

...now who will tell you exactly which one to choose and why?

A large majority of people make their decisions by looking at what the largest majority of people do (read that again and do the math).

This is a normal reaction to doubting your inner authority.

After all, if a million people all seem to do the same thing, it's more likely to be right.

The only flaw in the system is that those people are all looking at everyone else too.

Some people see through this, so they pick a counterculture that rebels against the mainstream ideology.

And then behave exactly the way a typical person of that counterculture would.

We call this "rebellious" and "authentic".

Like anarchists who have to follow all the endless rules of anarchism.

Punk rockers who are not allowed to look like an average joe.

Or spiritual people, who must take pride in how little ego they have.

Others might turn to motivational speakers or read a book for answers.

(But hopefully not one of those annoying books that tell you the choice is up to you and you'll do whatever you want to do.)

A big part of the reason we look at others to tell us what to do is this:

If it doesn't turn out well in the end, we can blame that person (or culture) for it.

When we make our own decisions, we can no longer do that.

Luckily, you already know that blame is an illusion and should not be confused with responsibility.

So you don't need anyone to make your decisions anymore.

You can claim back your freedom and power.

They're yours to use.

—"...OK, now what?

Can someone please tell me what to best use my freedom and power for?"—

Even after we claim back our power; most of us continue to seek some kind of guidance.

Because we want security. We want ease.

We want someone who has walked the path before and can tell us *"this is the way that is 100% safe and certain and fun".*

But most people's path was neither safe nor certain.

And more importantly, they have only walked *their* path, not yours.

So by blindly following them, you actually become less safe and certain compared to just exploring your own path one step at a time with full awareness of how the world responds to your steps.

Most of the questions we seek to answer —the things we want guidance with —are things nobody can answer with certainty.

So the best advice I can give you is to practice your capacity for being with uncertainty as it arises.

For being with insecurity and tension. And for calmly considering a large number of options without feeling the pressure to choose the right one.

Because there is no right one.

"Right" is an illusion too.

Every choice only exists as a potential until it is made.

The moment you act on your decision, one of those potentials becomes manifest and the others disappear.

So the only choice that ever really exists is the one you made.

And once you made it, there's no point in questioning whether it was right.

There's no way to know what would've happened had you made a different one.

Calling this one right or wrong doesn't change the fact that it's the one that happened.

The only choice which became real.

And it became real, because it was what you wanted to do.

How did you know you wanted to? Because you found yourself choosing it.

You may be fond of the outcome or not, but that's irrelevant when it comes to the choice.

Since the outcome was more than just a linear result of this decision.

It was a collaborative result of every other movement every wave in the ocean made that helped move yours until now.

Your choice was just a small ripple among many.

But it was the right one.

Because you made it.

Yes, having someone direct you towards "the right choices" is easier.

But it's also dangerous.

When you look for external answers, they may come from benevolent guides who give it their best shot to guide you (with the limitation that they can only know what works for them, not you).

But at other times, you may get influenced by people consciously feeding you lies to indoctrinate you into their ideology, or motivate you to buy their stuff.

When you become comfortable with uncertainty, you will no longer feel a strong need for guidance.

Which doesn't mean guidance can not be of help to you anymore.

But it'll make you more discerning when it comes to whose guidance to accept.

You'll be less hookable for people's abuse and emotional slavery.

And you will be even more free, having transcended the limitation of always *needing* to know.

"People will do anything, no matter how absurd, in order to avoid facing their own souls. They will practice Indian yoga and all its exercises, observe a strict regimen of diet, learn theosophy by heart, or mechanically repeat mystic texts from the literature of the whole world—all because they can not get on with themselves and have not the slightest faith that anything useful could ever come out of their own souls."

— Carl Jung

Society is a massive meta gameworld in which one of the goals is finding a way for humanity to thrive and coexist together.

One process through which this is attempted is people coming up with proposed rules for the gameworld and trying to get everyone to agree to them.

People will say:

- *"This is what's okay in a relationship and what is not."*
- *"This is how many hours we should work."*
- *"These are the Gods we believe in."*

The more people they get to enroll in the rules they're creating, the more ideological real estate their proposals take up in the gameworld of society.

This is one of the many ways we hide our freedom and power:

We accept someone else's rules and follow them, including their rule 0.

Suddenly we find ourselves unable to wear socks with sandals, even though it's rather comfortable

In the game of society, sometimes following these senseless rules and pretending they are real is necessary.

Because society is something we can't play alone. And we sure can't figure out the full details of how everything works by ourselves.

But it's important to know that whatever rules you subscribe to aren't necessarily the actual rules of reality.

It's second hand information you temporarily choose to agree with.

And you are the one exercising your own power by following them.

So if you in your heart of hearts disagree with a rule, remember that you are powerful and free.

You don't have to accept someone else's rulebook. You can find people willing to co-create a new one.

That is, if you can deal with the temporary confusion and dizziness of the period in between during which rules don't seem to exist.

And of course, handle the possibility that their rule was a necessary one, but you just didn't understand what was so good about it

Even then, it's through questioning the rule that you discover its value.

Which is a much more helpful process than blindly agreeing to what's presented to you.

You wouldn't sign a contract without reading it, would you?

Question everything, but don't discard it.

You can live life on your own terms.

If you let go of the desire for someone to tell you what to do and how to do it right.

If you let anyone tell you how to live, let it be life itself.

Because no matter what you do, life is always talking to you.

In a very real and direct way.

If you're willing to listen.

CHAPTER 23
YOUR PURPORTED PURPOSE

A funny thing happens to us when we reclaim our own freedom, power and sovereignty.

No longer having to answer to anyone, finally realizing that we can be the authority in our own life, we may be faced with a sudden question:

What's my purpose here?

A question that is important indeed. Because what's freedom in a life without meaning and purpose? A slippery slope to nihilism and debauchery.

Yet at the same time, there's a glaring irony in finally claiming your identity as an adult who can make their own decisions, only to immediately make "your life purpose" your new daddy.

For some people, not knowing their life purpose is a constant source of agony.

It freezes them to the point where they feel they can't do anything until their purpose is clear.

Or it shifts them into high gear. Not resting until they identify it.

They will travel to the Himalayas and the heart of the Amazon hoping to get a clue about what to do with their lives.

This, my friend, is exactly what disowned anxiety looks like.

This is the dizziness of freedom.

If your life has a divine purpose, something you were put on this earth to do, wouldn't it stand to reason that you are already fulfilling it in ways you may not understand?

If there was a point to all of it —which there might very well be— wouldn't that mean everything life is doing *to* you, doing *through* you or doing *with* you, would honor that divine purpose in some way?

What makes your heart beat?

What makes your lungs breathe?

What gives you great ideas?

If all these parts of life run on their own without having to think about them, and if there truly is some bigger purpose to your existence, then how could you ever escape it?

It would be happening on its own accord, like the rest of your life.

Even if you knew your purpose, and consciously (or should I say "on purpose"?) tried to do the opposite, that might turn out to be part of the divine plan all along.

So why worry about it?

If you do have a purpose, then it's already steering your behavior.

In which case there's no need to find it.

But if you don't have a purpose then you can't find it.

In which case there's no need to go look for it.

Finding your "true passion" or "life's purpose" are big, dramatic projects.

And how would you even know when you've found them?

Without a black on white Certificate of Purpose™ handed to you by the universe and signed by baby Jesus, how can you ever be 100% certain?

Trying to latch on to your purpose in a two phrase mission statement only serves to distract you from the dizziness of freedom.

What if instead, you focus on the little nudges your intuition is sending you?

Little hints of excitement and curiosity.

Hints that something might not be good for you.

Topics you feel drawn to study.

Side quests that keep attracting you.

And trust that they're all leading you somewhere which you do not understand yet.

Each apparent detour or delay offers unique learnings and opportunities that a linear path (if such a thing exists) would not hold.

Embark on projects you're inspired to work on and abandon them when you get the sense they're no longer a good fit.

Don't fall prey to the narrative that you should finish everything you started.

Finish the things you care about, and investigate why you care so much about them.

Make very few promises and keep the ones you made.

Maintain relationships for the sake of the people in them and the connection between them, not because on paper it's something you "must do".

Trust that honoring these intuitions is taking you somewhere.

Because if it is, the dots will likely only connect in hindsight.

And if it isn't, at least you will have had a great time doing stuff that you enjoyed doing.

Learning things because you're coerced to is hard every step of the way.

Learning things because you're curious is hard to stop.

Maybe your life has a purpose, maybe it doesn't.
Either way, you're fulfilling it.

So now that you are here.

Now that you can't *not* follow your purpose and are allowed to do anything you want.

Now that you possibly have no clue what to do but know that you'll do the right thing anyway (because whatever choice you make is the right one).

Now what?

Now you find love.

Love in what's here.

Love in what you are.

Love in what you choose to do, rather than its projected outcome.

Now you get to play the game of hide and seek.

Learn to notice when you're hiding a bit too well again.

Congratulate yourself for your performance, reveal yourself as the source of love and have a celebration.

The idea that right now *"you are exactly where you need to be doing what you need to do, so you can just let go"* can be comforting to hear for many.

But rather than just entertaining it, consider it deeply for a moment:

What if it's true?

What if you accepted that idea deeply on a cellular level.

That there's nothing you ever have to do.

How would you feel about yourself?

Honestly, for me personally, the answer is *"not always that great"*.

My ego feels a lot better when I make myself believe that there's stuff I *have* to work on.

Things to improve.

Which brings up a worthwhile inquiry:

Ever wondered why you want yourself (or your surroundings) to be better than you are today?

Is it pure excitement about what's calling you? Or is it to get away from your present self (or surroundings) as they are?

Here's the question:

If everything would stay exactly the way it is right now, forever.

How would you feel about that?

Could you love that version of yourself fully?

Could you find the love within everything that surrounds you?

And knowing that no activities could possibly lead to any form of improvement, would any activities inspire you as an expression of pure play again?

CHAPTER 24

IT APPEARS WE HAVE A DOUBLE BOOKING

— *"Hold on... Let's rewind a bit.*

- *I can't do anything that goes against my life purpose.*
- *No matter how I feel, it's love in disguise.*
- *Resistance isn't real and all my excuses are valid.*
- *I am always following my real priorities .*
- *I'm always busy achieving my real goals.*

Then on what basis can I still make a clear decision what to do?"
—

You just do anything you want, as long as you do it without intending to cause harm to anyone.

—*"Alright then, smartiepants. What if the things I do are acts of self-sabotage?*

How could that still be doing what I want?"

My friend, you're never sabotaging yourself.

You're just trying to succeed at two things that seem to be in conflict with each other.

Remember how we talked about quitting smoking?

And how quitting will automatically happen when you want it more than *not* quitting?

The same is true of a lot of the things we call "hard to do".

If you look at them in a practical sense, they are extremely easy to do.

Break a habit? Easy, stop doing it.

Start a habit? Easy, start doing it.

Resist a temptation? Easy, don't act on it.

The reason they feel hard to us is because we have competing commitments.

A temptation is only tempting when a part of us wants it and another part doesn't.

If we are fully committed to not doing it, we can't be tempted.

If we are fully committed to doing it, it's not a temptation.

It's the thing we were already going to do.

The reason your own behavior can look like self-sabotage is that one of your competing commitments is hidden from you.

We may think we cheated on the diet we had committed to, but what really happened is we honored the pleasure and comfort we were *also* committed to.

By consuming seventeen chicken nuggets and a tub of ice cream, our soul invited our attention towards that commitment.

It's saying:

"Hello, dear madam/sir.

Seems like one of your commitments was being kept in the dark.

Would you like to shine some light on it?

So that you may understand it better and learn to honor it more effectively?"

What seems like behavior we didn't want to engage in but for some reason did anyway, is often behavior we *wanted* to engage in but didn't understand why.

There's always a payoff behind what we do.

And if we understand that payoff, we can use the "shortcut" principle from chapter 2 to meet it in a more effective way.

Perhaps one that is not in conflict with our other commitments.

If you find it hard to let go of:

- a habit you think doesn't serve you

- a perpetual unpleasant thought cycle

- a situation you know you better leave

Then ask yourself: *"What am I getting out of this that I'm not seeing?"*

Sometimes it can be as obvious as *"I don't like my job, but I do it because a predictable income stream feels safe and that's important to me"*.

Sometimes it can be as far-fetched as having a victim story to elicit care from the outer world or publicly justify behavior we otherwise wouldn't get away with.

The payoff for everything we do can be distilled down to the belief that it will help us find love and safety.

Once you see that, you will see how none of your commitments are truly in competition with each other at all.

For example:

I am committed to seeing others through the eyes of compassion, yet sometimes my thoughts are harsh and judgmental.

Why? Because I'm also committed to self-worth.

And when I feel less worthy, judging others gives my ego an inflated sense of righteousness and superiority.

On a superficial level, it may seem like these commitments are in conflict.

But they are not. They are both commitments to love.

If I viewed myself with the same compassion I intend to view others with, I would no longer judge others that harshly.

In my experience, a great way to reconcile competing commitments is talking to yourself in the mirror

To look yourself in the eyes and ask:

"Why do you want to do these things?"

Then keep the conversation going until you find the love within.

If you try this, it's important that you do it with the intention of listening to yourself and fostering understanding. Not to *"get rid of one of the commitments"*.

Because the commitment is always a longing for love.

And trying to stop yourself from something that matters to you is the opposite of feeling the love you're trying to find.

For me the occasional mirror conversation works wonders (but maybe that's because I'm such a sexy beast and very enjoyable to look at).

For you it might be something else.

You might work with a specialized therapist who maps out all your different subpersonalities and moderates healing conversations between them.

Or you may find that simply recognizing that both commitments are a form of love playing hide and seek is already enough of a golden thread to bring you back to it.

Once you're aware of the love within them, your commitments no longer appear to be competing at all.

Because you embraced the fact that in the end, they're all attempts to serve the same agenda.

And whatever you end up doing —without the intent of harm— is what you wanted to do most.

"What happens if you start to see all those moments of self sabotage as wisdom you don't yet understand?

What if there is a subconscious intuition in you saying `no, this isn't right for me, not this...`, despite your conscious mind's best attempts to cling to it?"

Scott Domes

Sometimes what seems to be a case of competing commitments is just us thinking love is hiding somewhere other than where we are.

The cure to FOMO is accepting that you chose to do the thing you're doing.

No one is forcing you to.

You're doing the thing because you care more about what this means to you than the other thing.

This is a choice of love.

Yes, there's also love to be found in the thing you think you're missing out on.

But the easiest place to find love is right here.

With you and the option you chose.

CHAPTER 25

JIMMY WANTS YOUR MARGARITA (AND YOU WANT HIS DESIRE)

—*"But what if I don't know what I want?"*—

Then that's great news!

As you may remember: many of our wants are merely projections of our desire for love and safety.

So you won't have to deal with the popular self-torture of telling yourself you want to achieve something and then working really hard for it, only to notice that at the end of that rainbow is another pot of projected desires.

But if you find yourself asking the question: *"What should I do when I don't know what I want?"*, this reveals that deep down, you already do know what you want.

What you want is to want something. Anything.

Because you currently feel a sense of discomfort which you desire to escape from.

So if you could only discover something to want, you could start seeing that thing as your ticket out of the discomfort. As your Savior. The place where you convince yourself love is hiding.

But what if you choose not to answer the question?

And instead continue not knowing what you want?

When you have the sense that you want something but you don't know what it is, you are —in fact— closer to the core of your desire than those who do think they know.

Because those who know what they want still believe their projections to be the thing that will fix their life.

But you, in your not knowing, are closer to the feeling of your true desire.

So I invite you to sit with that feeling for a bit.

See if you can find the golden thread in it.

—*"How can I better understand myself?—*

How can you better understand anyone?

Through curious conversation and attentive listening.

There's this myth going around that people who talk to themselves are crazy.

But I suspect the opposite is true:

What if it's the people who never connect with themselves that slowly grow insane?

Take this theory with a grain of salt, as I don't have any data to back it up.

But in the meantime, it might not hurt to have the occasional chat with yourself, right?

If we want someone to feel safe to open up to us, the best way to go about it is to listen with deep, devotional attention.

Not to ask intrusive questions or expect revealing answers, but to offer your nonjudgmental presence as a listener.

Most advice about interpersonal relating, can also be applied to relating with ourselves.

Instead of probing and prodding yourself, saying *"What do you want? Tell me, so I can fix this!"*, can you just *be* with yourself?

Can you be the kind of friend to yourself that doesn't judge you for anything you might open up about?

Can you be the kind of friend to yourself who loves you as much on your worst days as on your best ones?

Can you be the kind of friend to yourself who doesn't fill the space with words but instead offers a hug, lets you cry on their shoulder and takes you out for something they know always makes you laugh?

Be the kind of friend to yourself that can be trusted to listen, help out and always has your best interests in mind?

Soon enough, you may hear yourself revealing exactly what you want.

Even if it doesn't match what you're "supposed" to, what you thought was "proper", or what you thought you liked.

In fact, that might be exactly why you've never told yourself before.

You were waiting until you could trust you'd be open enough to listen without arguing.

You're supposed to feel lost sometimes.

Like nobody's guidelines fit your path.

Like you can't predict where you'll be in one year.

It means you're taking the leap.

From illusion to reality.

From rigidity to freedom.

What if uncertainty is just a shadow of omnipotentiality?

Why do you want to want something?

If you finally would discover what it is you want in this life, what would that give you?

Direction.

Clarity.

A solution to the dizziness of freedom.

This is why it's so much easier to have someone tell us what to do.

Even if we claim our freedom and power as self-led, sovereign individuals, we're still secretly hoping to be led by *something*.

We like to pretend we're calling the shots, but deep down we're waiting for some sort of wanting, needing or purpose to arise within us. So we can follow *that*.

We do want to be directed.

We do want clarity to be *handed to us* by someone or something.

But we want the glory of believing it was us who came up with it.

If you want direction, here's how to get it:

A) Pick a direction. Any one. After all, all that's required for having direction is choosing one.

B) Trust that something greater is leading you and has wisdom you don't understand (whether that's your daddy, your desires or your deity).

If you want clarity, here's how to get it:

Don't do anything.

Wait. Stay open and attuned.

Be a space for life to move through.

Become the thing the moment calls for.

Witness the miracle that you are.

Take up your place as a wave for the ocean to move.

If you want this life to be yours, give yourself to it.

If you want life to give you clear directions, you must allow yourself to be moved by it.

It's hard for an ocean to make waves without the water cooperating.

The desire to want something is the desire to force your own growth.

But what if instead of pushing your own wave forward, you allowed the ocean to carry it?

Be a calm wave for a while.

Sit in your wantlessness.

It's something many people wish they had.

Monks spend years attempting not to want stuff.

Jimmy from down the street dreams of a tropical retreat.

Margaritas on the beach and zero activities scheduled for the rest of his life.

In other words: He wants to be in a place where he no longer wants anything else than to be there.

And if you don't want anything right now, you're already in that place.

You can enjoy this paradise!

All you need to do is get used to the dizziness that accompanies your freedom.

As you remain open to life's movements, eventually a want will arise.

"What's that... hunger?"

Can you hear what the hunger is for?

Pancakes?

Rib-eye?

Pumpkin pie?

Why not spend some time cooking it? After all, you don't have much else on your mind!

If the answers aren't clear, slow down and sharpen your senses.

Soon you'll find that in some periods, you barely find time to sit in silence.

Because you hear life's messages clearly, every minute of the day.

—*"But what if I never end up wanting anything at all?*

Won't I just spend my life waiting forever?"—

Well in that case, you have two options (the same you always have):

You can either do something or do nothing.

If you do something and you find out it wasn't what you wanted, then you're one step closer to wanting something.

Because you know you want something different than that.

And if you do nothing, you can be proud of yourself.

It's quite the achievement.

Everyone who's too busy says they crave a moment to do nothing.

Then when people finally have it, they say *"please tell me what to do, I'm bored"*.

How much of what you want or need is merely a contract you made with yourself?

"As long as I don't have this, I choose not to be comfortable with myself."

Without these contracts in place, you might notice the discomfort is still there.

But if you spend enough time sitting with it, you'll become quite acquainted, quite intimate with it.

And what feels more comfortable than spending time with an intimate friend?

Celebrate it. Be glad that you get to do nothing.

I've personally tried and failed many times.

—*Seriously though... What if I do that, and I never end up wanting anything anymore?* —

In the rare event that it happens (trust me, the chance is small), you'll have achieved what some people have tried to achieve for thousands of years: Transcending desire itself.

The last freedom.

To be so free that you don't even need the freedom anymore.

Don't worry about it.

Do nothing. Do something.

Let life decide for you.

Or pretend you're the one running the show (even though that's possibly just life deciding it wants you to pretend to be running it).

All roads lead to Rome.

Anything can show you the way to love if you allow it to.

CHAPTER 26

YES MEANS NO (BUT NO DOESN'T MEAN YES)

There's a lot of fear-mongering in the self-help-o-sphere.

People say things like: *"If you don't have a clear goal, you'll be used by someone else to achieve theirs."*

Don't let such ideas get to you.

You have power. You have freedom. You have agency.

Just because you don't know what you want doesn't mean others can use you.

Nobody can use you without your cooperation.

And yes, sometimes we may cooperate with things we don't feel good about.

But that's exactly what you need when you don't know what you want.

Those things can then point the way to what we *do* feel good about. Showing you what it is you *do* want.

If you don't know what you want, then life is basically one big breakfast buffet.

You can walk around, take a bite of everything, discover how you respond to it and say:

"I like this, I want more like it." or *"I don't like this, I'll leave it on the table."*

Ever experienced a situation where you said "yes" to something you didn't fully want?

Most of us have. For a variety of reasons:

- Out of worry for not being able to handle the repercussions (not feeling safe).
- To avoid disappointing others or hurting their feelings.
- To avoid conflict or confrontation.
- To reciprocate past favors.
- To procure future favors.

Sometimes it can be as simple as not having a specific reason to say no.

This has long been a personal struggle of mine:

If there's no strong reason to say no, I thought, why be annoying? Just say yes.

But "yes" isn't as innocent as it appears to be.

You may think "yes" is a great guy because everybody loves hearing about him.

But honestly, he's kind of a dick.

He just has great PR.

Truth is: Everything you worry "no" does, "yes" does a million times more.

That may sound like an exaggeration. But it is not.

Let's examine exactly how it works:

"Yes" and "no" are both words which express a decision.

Whether it's about boundaries, proposals, ideas, requests, ...

Whenever you use these words, you use them to decide:

*"I want **this**, not **that**."*

Etymologically, making a *de-cision* means to cut off.

So whenever you use the words "yes" or "no", you are making a decision and therefore cutting something off.

Each time you say no to something, you are cutting off the possibility of making that thing happen.

Every 2 year old knows this. That's why they don't like to hear the word "no" from their parents

But what most people rarely think about, is that every time you say yes to something, you are cutting off *all other possibilities in existence at the same time.*

For example:

If your neighbor invites you to an activity you wouldn't enjoy, and you say no, you stop that activity from entering your reality.

But if you say yes to your neighbor's proposal of watching paint dry in his apartment, then you are effectively saying no to an infinite list of other things that could've happened.

In other words:

"No", just means no.

But "yes" means no multiplied to infinity minus one.

The idea that every yes is a million "no's" is not just philosophically true.

It's true in a practical way

Saying yes to everything will eventually lead to either having to say no to things you care about (because you committed to something random) or having to disappoint the people you said yes to (because you don't keep your commitments to them).

So if you are afraid of saying no, you should be way more afraid of saying yes.

So afraid that in comparison, "no" becomes the safest option for any situation,

Unless your whole body informs you that yes is better.

If you're willing to be unreasonable, no one can use reason to manipulate you into saying "yes" to something you don't want.

A true yes shines so brightly it illuminates the shadows of the million no's it created.

It says yes to something you truly want.

So much that if someone were to give you a print-out of all the exact things your yes is causing you to say no to, you would still consider it a good choice

True yesses are shared at the start of adventures, screamed during orgasms and stammered at altars while tears of joy ruin the most overpriced makeup of a lifetime.

Not sadly whispered, staring at the floor while a parent scolds you, awkwardly smiled at a co-worker's creepy joke, or politely spoken out of social obligation.

So next time you're about to say yes to something out of habit, out of fear, or for any other reason really, try and remind yourself:

"Unless this is something I want with every fiber of my being, my yes is mostly a million no's.

And I'm pretty scared of no's. Let alone a million of them.

So how about we just stick to one simple no and call it a day?"

If you accidentally end up saying yes to something you don't want, don't worry

Ask yourself: *"Why did I say yes?"*

The answer shouldn't surprise you: You said yes because you wanted to.

Maybe you had a competing commitment to pleasing others or to avoid "rocking the boat".

If you did, remember: That commitment is there because you believe it'll help you locate love.

Just like saying no to this thing and yes to something else would've been.

And if either of those commitments take you away from love too often, they'll lead you back to favoring the other option.

You can't do it wrong.

Because if you do, doing it wrong is what eventually shows you how to do it "right".

And you may find that wrong was a necessary step for you in learning exactly what "right" means to you.

Every time you find yourself regretting you said yes is a great opportunity to get to know yourself better:

Why did you want to say yes?

Was it to make an impression?

Was it to maintain a positive relationship?

Was it to end a conversation you experienced as stressful?

Talk to yourself and listen without judgment.

Seek to understand your competing commitments.

Understand how, deep down, they're all expression of the same one:

An unwavering commitment to caring for yourself.

Everything that seems like an act of self-sabotage is just another act of love.

Sneaking by in disguise. Barely able to contain its excitement that one day you'll find out where it was hiding.

—*"But if I just walk around through life saying no to everything others want, and yes only to what I want...won't that make me a bad person?"*—

If you're asking that question, I can say with certainty that you are not a bad person.

After all, the question is an expression of care for yourself and others.

And you're right, this life isn't lived in separation. You're not the only wave in the ocean.

And you may find it's sometimes hard to say where one wave ends and another begins.

But if you'd allow every other wave in the ocean to completely engulf you, you would no longer be able to move freely.

Which includes not being able to move in ways that benefit others.

The stronger your boundaries, the more generous you can be.If you give yourself ample space to move as you desire, you might just become one of the waves that lift up the rest of the tide.

The conversations in this book have been quite self-centered indeed.

But that's for a reason:

Interpersonal relationships could be a great topic for a future book, but your relationship with yourself sets the tone for all of them.

It's the foundation on which all connections are built.

Because no matter who you interact with, *you* will be there too.

Even questions about morality —and their answers— can often be traced back to your relationship with yourself.

CHAPTER 27
THE STAIRCASE OF MORALITY

"Right is right even if no one is doing it.
Wrong is wrong even if everyone is doing it."

— St. Augustine

Even when we realize we have the power and freedom to make our own choices and there's no one telling us what to do, our minds still have a last resort tactic for trying to put the responsibility on someone else's shoulders: Outsourcing the morality behind our choices.

We might ask some certified holyman to tell us whether it's okay to punish our kids, marry someone of the same gender or fantasize about the girl next door.

Or perhaps as a more recognizable example, we might say:

"Sure, technically pirated music is stealing, but everyone's doing it, so... ...yeah."

But just as you can't outsource power and responsibility, you can't outsource your morality.

A million people might tell you something is a proper moral choice, but you are still the one deciding to agree with them.

One of the eternal debates about morality is whether there is such a thing as good and evil.

Is morality absolute or is it all relative?

Whenever we try to force ourselves to choose between two polar opposites, we fail to notice all the nuance in the middle.

Moral absolutism can't be all there is. Because it completely ignores the context and intention behind a person's actions.

When Robin Hood steals money from an oppressive tyrant and gives it to their struggling subjects, most of us have a gut feeling that this isn't as immoral as robbing a jewelry store to pay for your cocaine habit.

Realizing that morality isn't black and white comes with the perceived burden of figuring out exactly which shade of gray something is.

So it can be tempting to relieve ourselves of that burden by swinging in the other direction and concluding there's nothing good or bad except for how we look at it.

But let's be honest: Seeing child abuse as a morally positive would require such challenging mental gymnastics that there's little doubt about it being an immoral thing.

Both moral relativism and moral absolutism are yet another attempt at denying our own power and responsibility.

Moral absolutism does so by giving us a rulebook for our choices.

Now we no longer need a leader. We are "free" to make choices, but we use that freedom to follow a set of rules which tell us exactly what to do.

Moral relativism, on the other hand, pretends to liberate you. But all it does is shrink down the list of commandments to one, being:

"When your intuition informs you something is immoral, ignore it. Because it's all relative."

In other words, it robs you of the freedom and power to listen to your own moral discernment by having you believe morality doesn't exist.

I do believe that intrinsic morality exists.

A morality that is already present inside all of us.

And that the calibration of our moral compass is directly tied to our awareness of love in the present moment.

When the presence of love is obvious to us, we will act in service of good.

There is no ulterior motive to our goodness. It just is.

But when we fail to spot where love is hiding, our morality becomes one of manipulation.

A morality in which goals justify the means, and we use whatever means we are able to rationalize using.

The harder it is for us to perceive love's presence, the more twisted our morality becomes.

As love disappears from our awareness, we descend down the "staircase of morality".

Where the top of the staircase would be:

- Intrinsic morality (Good for goodness sake)

The next steps down are:

- Morality out of care for others and our environment
- Rational morality (*"I'll behave the way I'd want everyone to behave, to contribute to the kind of world I'd love to live in."*)
- Morality for self-esteem's sake (*"I did a good deed. Am I not a great moral?"*)
- Morality for personal gain (*"In the long-term, being good always pays."*)
- Morality for status (*"It's important that people notice how good I am."*)
- Morality out of fear (Of going to hell, of being punished, of losing a relationship,...)

All of these might lead to doing the right thing, just not out of intrinsic morality.

But that's not a problem per se, as the actions they lead you to take might still make you discover the intrinsic morality within you.

Because from each of these steps, you can still see the step above it and move towards it if you wish.

However, when we reach a point where love feels entirely absent to us (not coincidentally, the same point at which our emotions can turn destructive too), morality as a concept stops existing in our experience.

First we get to:

- Moral relativity (*"Nothing is good or bad, it all depends how you look at it."*)

Which, as we've seen, can be experienced as the illusion of liberation. But in reality, it robs you of the freedom to make moral choices.

More importantly, moral relativity is the first step on the staircase at which you're in the dark.

It no longer allows you to recognize the existence of the steps above it, because it says they are not real.

Increasing the likelihood that you'll descend further down the staircase, rather than climb back up.

Unfortunately, further down, things start to get a lot darker.

Because on the bottom of the staircase we find:

- Morality out of shame (*"I'm bad and I should be good, but I seem incapable of it."*)
- Immorality out of victimhood (*"It's a dog eat dog world. You gotta take what you can get."*)
- Inverted morality (*"Good and bad don't exist. Therefore it's wisest to do anything you can for your personal gain. Which makes you superior to those stupid people acting all docile based on false limiting beliefs about morality."*)
- And finally, pure immorality (Acting evil for evil's sake.)

So if you ever find yourself in the seductive realms of moral relativity, may this chapter remind you that the top of the staircase *does* exist.

And the bottom doesn't lead to much good for anyone who goes there.

If you ever do find yourself on the dark side out of the staircase of morality, remember:

To find the way up, you can always follow the golden thread love left for you.

Here's some examples of where you might find it:

Moral relativity is a belief arising from a deep longing to be free. And that longing is where love is hiding.

Shame-based morality looks for love through the acceptance you might one day receive from others, from yourself, or from the divine (as seen in catholic shame-based morality).

Inverted morality is a perverse expression of self-love.

Because if you weren't full of unfelt love for yourself, why would you desire to take from others so you could feel it? Your love for yourself is what makes you care about feeling loved.

The very force driving you to fill that big empty hole in your soul, is secretly the force that the hole is already filled to the brim with

Waiting for you to find it in yourself. To feel it. And to win this game of hide and seek.

Even pure immorality has a tiny golden thread in it

Because no matter how much I wish I didn't exist, the love of evil is still love.

Love with evil as its object of reverence.

Which means that by some miracle of God, it might still be possible for that same love to change its focus. To realize that love was the power the person experienced, and evil just the point of attention.

That the golden thread can still theoretically be followed towards morality, perhaps even redemption, but turning love's point of attention towards itself again.

What makes an action good or bad?

One interpretation of a "good action" could be an action that doesn't harm others

Another could be that it serves the greater good, regardless of what it looks like when viewed from a smaller perspective?

But since everything's part of the same interconnected ocean, it's unlikely that our human mind could correctly ascertain what *exactly* serves the greater good and what doesn't.

What if an assassination attempt on a corrupt leader inspires them to do better?

What if the extreme horrors of a war traumatize humanity to such a degree they'd rather reconcile their differences than ever repeat it?

What if the generosity from one party towards another leaves their benefactor with a sense of entitlement, or takes away the drive for learning to meet their own needs?

Of course, in all these examples, the opposite is just as possible.

We cannot control the full impact of our actions But there's two things we can control:

Our intention and our awareness

When you're self-aware and honest with yourself, you can feel your true intentions

No matter how pretty (or ugly) they look on paper.

The content of your actions may indeed be neutral but your intention can make it positive or negative.

And what your intention is will depend on how aware you are of the love all around you.

How good you are at playing hide and seek.

When you connect to the love in your heart, you know right from wrong

Not in an absolute or binary sense. But in a specific to the moment sense.

Because when love is not lost to you, morality isn't either

And when love's hiding spot gets more obscure, so does your morality.

When you give a compliment, you can feel in your heart whether it was intended as:

- a gift of love for the other
- an attempt to bait them into giving love back to you
- an investment you hope creates goodwill from them (securing long-term love)

This is a perfect example of how we can discern our morality in a specific moment.

And if the intention behind an action isn't of "the highest step on the staircase", no need to judge yourself for it (that would only lead you down).

Remember:

The golden thread is discovering how deeply you must care about yourself to have any kind of intention meant to magnify the presence of love in your life.

When you allow yourself to reconnect to your most loving intentions, how could you ever take actions that cause harm on another unless it was truly a "punch a puppy or die" situation ?

Many might argue with this, saying:

"Well what about communist dictatorships? Isn't that an example of evil done with loving intentions?

But that's confusing proclaimed intentions with **real** intentions.

Just as a lover might say *"I'm only trying to keep you safe"* when their real intention is to control you, a government might say *"I'm trying to re-distribute wealth from the few to the many"* when it's glaringly obvious that every action is about re-distributing power and resources from the many to the few

Your mind might come up with all kinds of appealing stories of what your intentions are, but your heart always knows.

If you can't get yourself to do it with an open heart, don't do it with a closed one.

If your mind's wondering whether something is cheating, your heart already knows it is.

Remember: the best decisions are the ones your whole body agrees with.

When everyone around you has reasonable explanations why it's OK to do something, but your belly feels odd when you think about it, it's probably not OK to you.

Stay in touch with your intrinsic morality and use that to guide your actions, no matter:

- Who advised you
- Who ordered you to
- How many others do it

Not because of what others might think.

But because in your heart of hearts, you know what's good.

And you know when what you do is not.

—"But what if my heart tells me to do something immoral?"—

As long as you're in touch with love's presence, it won't.

Immoral choices are projections and manipulations.

They happen when we're losing the game of hide and seek?

Does anyone connected to love intrinsically want to steal?

No, but they do want to feel nourished and safe.

Does anyone intrinsically want to cross other people's sexual boundaries?

Not unless they forgot what love is (or believe they can't have it without this).

Did anyone intrinsically want to write a terrible script for the last 2 seasons of your favorite TV show? No, perhaps they just lost touch with the love for it.

Morality is not about good people vs. bad people.

It's about constructive vs. destructive states of being.

It's about being in service of, or in denial of love.

—"But what about trolley problems?

Don't they prove that morality is just one big gray area?"—

Like choosing between a bullet in the head or punching a puppy to death, the morality of trolley problems is actually the *easiest* to understand.

That is, if you stop trying to fix it.

The more impossible a moral dilemma is to resolve, the more likely that you don't need to worry about it.

You see, if the choice is between inflicting needless harm on someone or not doing so, the moral choice is obvious: Not doing so.

But when presented with 2 equally harmful choices, and being forced to choose one, then in the greater scheme of things, the only predictable consequences are somewhat equal in gravity.

So it all comes back to the same thing: Do whatever you want to do.

Yes, without the intent of harming someone. But the fact that you're actively trying to find the option which does as little harm as possible already reveals that that intent is there.

Remember, intention and awareness:

If you choose to kill a puppy to prevent being killed yourself, your intention was not to kill a puppy. It was to keep yourself alive.

And if your trolley problem was too complicated to have a clear answer, that means you lacked the awareness to predict which option most served the greater good.

Which is an awareness I imagine very few people have (if any).

So the best solution is to pick a random one and have compassion for yourself.

It's not easy being a railroad switch operator.

CHAPTER 28

FAST AND FURIOUS: DEALS WITH THE DEVIL

"In order to control myself I must first accept myself by going with and not against my nature."

— Bruce Lee

"Once you fire the manager in your head it will be unsettling.

But you can then open yourself up to things emerging at their own pace.

You no longer need to crush a goal in 2 months.

You can just steer attention in the direction and take small steps until things fall into place".

- Paul Milerd

When you move from one place to another or from one moment to the next, you can optimize for speed or optimize for presence.

The more you slow down, the more your senses can receive the gifts of the journey.

The more you speed up, the sooner you get to harvest the fruits of the destination.

Neither speed is a wrong way for you to be.

There are certainly places so far out of reach that going slowly means you won't ever get there.

Yet on the other hand, rushing through life is also rushing your arrival at the destination of death.

Speed expends more energy and blinds you to the details.

Ever been in a race car?

Once you go fast enough, the world outside the windshield is reduced to a blurry tunnel of color without texture.

The same thing happens when you race through life.

The months blur into years.

The speed rings in your ears.

And eventually you wonder: *"Where did all the time go?"*

It was optimized away.

"...and how did I get here?"

Your haste turned into haze.

"...and why am I so tired?"

Because the low fuel light's been on for hundreds of days.

But the tunnel vision kept blurring it away.

There are moments when speed is of the utmost essence.

In such moments you will be able to achieve the most speed if, up until then, you've kept a healthy balance between leisure and activity.

Between pausing to refuel and running the gears so they don't get rusty.

What do you do when one day your car doesn't feel like driving?

You take it to the workshop.

Now what if that happens a bit too often?

Then you figure out what you've been doing to your car that causes this.

Maybe you left the headlights on all night..

Maybe you forgot to check the tire pressure.

Or you drove in a higher gear than necessary.

Now what do you do when your mind doesn't feel like thinking?

When your body doesn't feel like carrying you?

Or when you lose the ability to empathize in relationships?

If you keep forcing yourself to function when you need care, you will eventually be forced to care when you need to function.

Force pretends to offer shortcuts.

But in reality, it offers delays.

Remember when we talked about shortcuts to your goals?

How knowing what your goal represents to you can reveal ways in which you could receive it faster?

Forceful action is the exact opposite of that.

It zones in on the goal as if achieving it in that specific form, by that specific deadline, is all that matters.

It pushes you to go faster, until the tunnel vision stops you from seeing the very thing you're after.

And while you're busy rushing towards the top of your mountain —where you believe you'll finally find love, freedom and all that you desire— you are blinded to the opportunities to receive them today.

That is the illusion of productivity.

It gets you to your projected goal faster, but postpones the reward that is the goal's purpose.

The illusion that you can force results to come faster is the essence of any deal proposed by the devil.

You want to feel good, so you binge on fast food. This triggers a quick release of dopamine and brings short-term satisfaction. But it also disrupts your hormones and brain chemistry, making it harder to feel good in the long run.

Take any devil's deal too frequently and it can create the opposite of what you're after: A reality of physical and emotional suffering.

Such a reality leaves you even more hungry for a short-term fix.

But the more you cave to this hunger, the more you fall into the devil's claws.

And unknowingly deliver on the contract's clause:

Your soul, enslaved to the pursuit of fleeting satisfaction while creating increasing amounts of self-inflicted suffering.

This is how the devil claims you.

And no matter where you are in life or how much you have, he'll always whisper in your ear attractive proposals to pacify your fears:

- *"Why wait on something that may never come when with a little force, you've already won?"*
- *"I know you're tired, my friend. But resting only makes the road longer. And it's the road that left you exhausted in the first place...so why not work a little harder?"*

If you listen to the whispers and force yourself despite needing a break, your ego's self-esteem inflates:

"I did the thing, God, I'm so great."

But the next day you're twice as tired and still didn't find what you were looking for.

Worst of all, you may now have achieved your goal while feeling no different from before.

So you must conclude: *"Seems like I'm not there yet, I have to try something else (or a lot more of the same)."*

And that is how the devil keeps you vexed.

The lesson here is not that speed is bad.

It's that trying to force yourself —or anyone else— to create a certain outcome faster than is natural will usually lead to the exact opposite of what you're trying to achieve.

While also creating the illusion that what you're doing is working.

Keeping you stuck in hell's hamster wheel.

Fueled by a fire that feels like motivation but is just a mask for existential fear.

Evil begins with the intention to force our surroundings to meet our needs.

This intention arises when we're impatient, or lack the faith that what's important to us will be taken care of.

We feel this way when we see the future as a relief from our dissatisfaction with the present.

That is why embracing the present can purify your soul.

And why rushing through life makes you more likely to sell it.

It's when I am impatient that I overwork and underlove.

That I spin my gears but don't go anywhere.

And spend my days like a top-tier achiever, but end them void of any meaning.

When we feel impatient, it means we have lost sight of love.

This gives us a sense of urgency and seriousness.

When in reality, it's rare for anything to be truly urgent.

I once saw a "gym bro" ignore his phone ringing for five sets in a row.

Upon which his spotter asked:

"Dude, aren't you going to answer that at some point?"

The bro replied in the most matter-of-fact tone possible, saying:

"Why? If someone died, they'll still be dead after my workout."

I'm still not sure whether that's deep wisdom or deep dumbassery.

But what I do know is that urgency is much more rare than we make it up to be.

Yet when we feel insecure, unworthy, unsafe or unloved, everything we believe could bring relief becomes *emotionally* urgent to us.

And that is when the devil seizes the chance to seduce us with convincing proposals presented as no-brainer deals.

When you hear such whispers, as enticing as they may sound, remember that love's always whispering too.

The voice of love might not always sound as loudly. But that's for a good reason:

If it makes too much noise, that wouldn't be a very loving way to tickle your ears.

And besides, betraying its hiding place like that would make it too easy for love to lose the game of hide and seek.

So whatever whispers are noisy and near, are most likely the devil's, my dear.

Look for the ones that are quiet and clear, because when you've identified those, that's when the golden thread appears.

And rescues you from signing a terrible deal.

—*"But how can I know for sure that patience will work and I'm not just procrastinating?"*—

How do you know anything will work?

You don't. You can't predict the future.

For a strategy to "work" implies that it can guarantee a certain outcome.

Which nothing can.

The illusion of using force is that it makes you feel more confident about your ability to influence the future.

Patience has nothing to do with action or inaction, but with your internal attitude towards the natural pace at which you alternate between both.

Whether you do something forcefully or patiently and gracefully, you're still doing it.

The main difference is that using force drains you of energy.

And allowing yourself the grace to go at your own pace increases your energy.

A wave will happen whether it tries to force itself into existence or instead relaxes and allows itself to be moved by the ocean.

But a patient wave will feel relaxed while moving, and an impatient one will feel tense.

Force can not make any outcome more certain than grace can.

In any case, the outcome will only be discovered when it comes out.

That's the only way for a potential to turn into a certainty.

Anything else is just creating the illusion of control to soothe yourself from the dizziness of freedom.

One of the few future outcomes we can predict with a high degree of certainty, is that the body will one day die.

Which is what makes being alive in it such a wonderful reason to celebrate.

Everything is always changing.

Knowing that no individual expression of life will last forever in the same form can be a strong inspiration to savor each moment with all your senses.

The more we remind ourselves of death, the more it can remind us to live.

In this sense, grief is a doorway to gratitude.

The deeper you embrace impermanence and loss, the deeper the gratitude that spontaneously arises.

To prevent falling for a devil's deal, develop a healthy relationship with life itself.

As with people, a lot of life's behavior will always be outside of your control.

And trying to control it often makes things worse.

As for the very small part of life that is *within* your control, do with it what feels authentic to you.

Don't overthink authenticity.

You are always as authentic as you have the capacity to be.

It's impossible not to be you.

The only thing that can change is the degree to which you are aware of it.

Are there degrees of authenticity?

Maybe.

Like when you align your soul, your actions and your speech.

But if there's a certain degree of "authenticity" that feels too much for you right now, then the most authentic thing to do is not force yourself to embody so much of it.

That's the paradox of authenticity.

There is nothing to do, but enjoy the games of hide and seek we play with ourselves.

And whether you're great at finding or great at hiding, both make you an essential part of love's game.

My favorite self-acceptance tool is "getting the joke" of the loop you're in.

For example:

By trying to be more self-accepting, you are not accepting the part of you that isn't.

Personal growth is full of such paradoxical jokes.

Once you see the joke of any personal growth pursuit, you realize that what you're trying to fix is an illusion.

And usually, that realization leads to the exact growth you were looking for in the first place.

But if you're trying to use the "find the joke technique" in an attempt to achieve this, then buckle up, because in that joke, you're the butt.

I've come to believe that the reason we so often get stuck in these apparent loops is that without the loop existing, the realization wouldn't occur to us.

How could you ever have a breakthrough without anything to break through?

Psychologists might scold me for this, but what if neurosis is just another fun game of hide and seek we play with ourselves?

"You won't achieve your goal until you give it 100% of your effort.", the success guru preaches.

Don't let their absolutist language fool you.

Take a day off.

Let it all hang out.

Flexibility is a great quality to cultivate.

It's actually required for most goals.

Because life's process won't bow or bend to your fancy plans.

Consistency is fetishized as the true secret to success.

But consistency doesn't guarantee any outcomes.

It only guarantees more of what you're doing.

If what you're doing feels good, good feelings will compound.

If it doesn't, stress will accumulate.

If what you're doing creates a consistent outcome, results will compound.

If it doesn't, dysfunction will.

Consistency is portrayed as never missing a day.

But that would mean you're missing all your days off.

A deal with the devil, because in the end, forced rest is all you'll get.

Remember, he key to consistency isn't choosing a frequency and forcing yourself to stick with it.

It's finding a frequency that's sustainable for you no matter what, then working to increase capacity over time.

It's a tough life trying to force a highly competent being into a rhythm that hinders its very strengths.

Stay attuned to your body and soul, that is the way to "effort less."

Discipline can come from two places: self-love and self-hate.

(Though as you might already guess by now, self-hate is just self-love that's very well hidden.)

Both look the same and give the same initial results.

You may not feel the difference.

But over time, discipline that comes from hate can lead to serious issues.

Here's how to tell them apart:

Self-hating discipline uses phrases like:

- *"I must do this every day."*
- *"Not doing it is not an option."*
- *"I'm a winner, unlike all those undisciplined losers."*

Love-based discipline uses phrases like:

- *"I choose to do this every day."*
- *"Taking days off is OK, it rejuvenates me."*
- *"Doing this is so obvious to me, that I barely think or talk about it."*

The key to moving from a rigid, self-hating form of discipline to a flow-like, effortless form of discipline is questioning where your goals come from.

Do you have these goals because you believe you should?

Because you believe that without achieving them, you won't be good?

Or were they born out of intrinsic excitement and curiosity?

You can only be lazy when you're mean to yourself.

If you subtract the meanness from your "laziness", what remains is restfulness.

The ideal routine is different every day, as your exact needs will rarely be the same.

But you'll find many similarities.

Observe which hours of the day you feel most energized, focused, creative or social.

Then design your schedule around those patterns.

This will help you flow more effortlessly with the way the ocean moves your wave.

But never stop listening.

If one day your rhythm is different, trust it.

Learn to dance with your nature.

The purpose of having a plan is to know very clearly what you're deviating from.

Remember: There's no such thing as a distraction.

Only what you choose to put your focus on.

Life plays out in mysterious ways.

When I follow my "distractions", they often lead me to something better than what I thought was so important to focus on.

But distractions tend to operate on a different time frame, that's why we don't notice their value.

Sometimes it's only years later that I realize: *"Oh, that side quest turned out to be essential to the main quest!"*

If something keeps calling your attention, it might be more important to you than you currently understand.

Trying to banish your thoughts of the future and past won't make you more present.

The trick is to be with them without giving them too much weight.

After all, they're part of the present moment too.

Your plan is a lay of the land of the future.

It's good to have a map at hand.

Just remember that the land of the future is flat-earthed.

You can only see until the edge.

You can imagine the kind of dragons or mystical cities lurking beyond the known horizon.

But once you sail past that point, what you encounter may be very different from the stories you had heard about it.

Some days, your map of the future is accurate.

And your vessel needs little tending to.

On such days, you can simply set sail and keep going straight.

But every morning, I've found it pays to check in at least:

What needs a little care in this body and soul?

What's alive in me today?

What's on my mind and heart?

What seems to call, inspire or excite me?

What course had I initially set for this day?

Is it still the wisest, with the current weather and morale of the crew?

Then you can decide on a new course and follow it until you don't want to anymore.

Maybe you were all in for skipping work today.

But then you realize you didn't wanna drift to financial ruin, so you showed up.

Or you felt a desire to sing your favorite song, but noticed while doing it, that it didn't feel as fun as you thought it would.

Keep checking in and adjusting your sails.

That's how you effortlessly sail with your own wave.

—"Should I go with the flow or create a solid structure?"—

Well my friend, it's impossible not to do both.

If you feel a desire for structure, planning and pushing, then that's exactly where the flow is taking you.

And if you feel a desire to let go, then letting go is the "structure" you created for your movement.

If the flow is taking you towards a desire to control and plan, then trying not to do that because *"you're committed to flowing"* ironically is a form of going against the flow.

But don't worry:

If you seem to be going against the flow, then that's just the way the flow invited you to dance today.

After all, who would like a leading dance partner that never allowed you to separate from them for a bit, make a beautiful twirl and fall back into their trustworthy hands?

You got this, you can't do it wrong.

A routine can liberate you or imprison you.

If you wake up in the morning and go for a walk because that's what you always do, the repetitive movement of the routine brings ease to the activity.

There is no decision making, you are moved by your own consistency.

But if you wake up and your body tells you it would be better to sleep a bit more, and you respond with *"no, I should never skip my morning walk!"*, then you have become a hostage of your own habits.

Sometimes the same things that initially empower or liberate us can become a prison over time.

So when you design a deliberately limiting structure (to enjoy the effortlessness that comes with a pre-designed plan), don't forget you left a note right here on this page of the book.

To read in case you ever feel stuck.

A note that says:

"If you find yourself trapped in a prison cell, don't go digging tunnels or trying to steal the keys.

Don't make deals with devils or beg for someone to release you.

You're the one who built this place.

It was you who made the blueprints. And you who forged the locks.

You're the inmate, the warden, the prison and the keys.

All of them simultaneously.

If you want to get out of your cell, get inside yourself.

Remember your role as the architect.

Remember this place doesn't really exist.

And build yourself a new home outside of it."

CHAPTER 29
THE PROCESS OF PERSONAL LIBERATION

— *"If it's true that whether I try to enforce change or not, things will always happen at the same pace, and that trying to rush them might even slow things down, then how can I ever get rid of these stubborn patterns that are holding me back?"*—

One of the implicit beliefs of the personal growth paradigm is that we should get rid of patterns and parts of ourselves that no longer serve us.

But why?

Why throw away something that was once very useful for your survival?

Imagine that as a child, you grew up in the wilderness.

You had to rely on hunting with a handcrafted spear to survive.

One day, you made it to the city.

Initially, whenever you got hungry in the city, you went out on the streets wielding your spear.

But you soon learned that the spear was working against you in this situation.

Instead of helping you get food, it got you kicked out of every store.

This is how all our seemingly unhelpful patterns originated.

They're metaphorical handcrafted spears.

At some point, they were an essential tool for our survival —or at least for our sanity.

But then the situation shifted and the same tools became detrimental to it.

Yes, it's possible to get rid of our metaphorical spears.

But wouldn't it be better to keep them in case a future situation ever called for it?

Wouldn't it be more appropriate to look at our spears with a feeling of gratitude rather than criticism?

What if you could keep all your past, present and future behaviors as tools on your belt, instead of demonizing some and glorifying others?

What that would look like in practice is that you wouldn't get rid of the pattern.

What you'd do is find a way to make it optional rather than compulsive.

Let's take an example from my own life, which I mentioned in the previous chapter: Overworking.

It's been a rather unhealthy pattern for me.

But it's also a great tool to have.

It's definitely better to have "overworking" as an option, than to not find yourself able to work extra hours if ever needed.

Just as "numbing your feelings" or "rebelling against the group" are patterns that can be harmful when you use them at all times, but very useful to have as an option.

Your entire personality is a collection of patterns.

Patterns that feel so natural and ingrained, you may not even realize they're tools you can put down and hang back on the belt whenever you want to.

Your "personality" is the sum total of behaviors and opinions you're addicted to.

It's perfectly possible to do the exact opposite of these at any point.

And you won't stop being you for doing so.

But it might make you a bit confused, as is always the case with newfound freedom.

Ever noticed how sometimes you seem to contain multitudes (or polar opposites) within yourself?

- Shy but outgoing?
- A laid back control freak?
- Kind but *"don't you dare mess with me"*?

That's because you do.

You contain the potential for every possible trait humans can have.

And your personality is a filter that decides how many of them you allow yourself to embody.

The vast majority of us humans are hypnotized by our own personalities.

We hypnotize ourselves into believing we are *"this way, but not that way"* by reciting stories, recalling memories and reaffirming the boundaries of our identity.

And we point to our own repetitive actions as proof that the attitudes behind them are inherent to us.

Once again, this comes down to dealing with the dizziness of freedom.

Just as we often look for external authority to tell us what to do, we create rules and patterns in our personalities that limit the options for how we allow ourselves to behave.

Because the more we limit our options, the more relief we find from the anxiety of having to choose our response in every moment.

When we have a personality trait that chooses *for* us, we don't need to feel the dizziness of freedom, nor the burden of responsibility.

Because it feels like our actions spring forth from a predetermined place, a personal nature which we can't transcend.

"Of course I did it that way, it's just who I am."

This is an amazingly efficient way of moving through life.

But unfortunately, it can't be achieved without creating a certain sense of stuckness or helplessness.

That's the flip side of the coin. We must hold an unshakeable belief that *"this is just the way I am"*, because if we would see past that illusion, we'd become aware of the infinite other choices we can make.

Which can slow down our functioning significantly.

That is why we need a personality in this world.

But make no mistake, It's still an illusion we hypnotize ourselves to believe is real.

And if you can liberate yourself from that, your options become limitless.

Just like we don't want to get rid of the patterns that hold us back but make them optional instead, I also wouldn't advise you to get rid of your personality.

I know many spiritual teachers preach ego death. But I can imagine you've grown quite fond of your personality. I know I have.

And if something brings you joy, why not keep it?

Why not keep your ego as a tool to hold in your hands —allowing you to use it quickly whenever you need it— but be aware you can hang it back on your belt, in case another tool would work better for the situation.

Personal freedom isn't as much the freedom of the persona to act, as it is allowing oneself to act free from the persona.

"*It is the person you imagine yourself to be that suffers, not you. Dissolve it in awareness. It is merely a bundle of memories and habits.*"

— Nisargadatta Maharaj

You can completely reinvent yourself in 24 hours.

If you're willing to let go of the likes, dislikes and patterns of your current personality, you can be reborn each morning.

Rehabilitate from who you think you are, and you'll find a freedom unlike anything you've ever known.

Let's take this one step further:

You are under no obligation to carry any energies from the previous moment into the next one.

You are absolutely allowed to shake it off, let go and arrive fresh into the reality of each new moment.

Look. Feel. Hear. Touch. Taste. Smell. Sense.

What's good about this moment?

By the time you've fully experienced it, it has already morphed into something new.

And so have you.

As you move from one moment to another, you may find a strong preference for behaving the same way as you did before.

To be consistent with the person you were a few minutes ago.

And there is nothing wrong with that.

As we've seen, a personality is a habit that helps us function in this world.

But there's a difference between choosing to act in accordance with it and being addicted to it.

If you felt a sudden impulse to do something that's the exact opposite of who you think you are (or should be), would you allow yourself to act on it?

When you let go of the need for being consistent with your persona, you become free to be as you are in each new moment. No matter what that turns out to be.

One word of warning though:

When you do, you may find that other people put pressure on you to fall back in line with your social identity:

- *"You're crazy."*
- *"You're inconsistent."*
- *"You're contradicting yourself."*

People often shame others for acting in ways that appear out of character because we all find emotional safety in the illusion of stability.

When someone allows themselves to be free beyond the limitations of their personality, that illusion is threatened. And we'll use blame or shame to reinforce it.

This makes sense.

Of course we'd rather spend time with someone who is predictably kind rather than someone who is kind one moment, then goes punching puppies the next.

So when people try to force you to act in accordance with their current understanding of who you are, do not see them as your enemy.

Just like you, they are seeking to create safety in our day to day reality.

With time, they might learn that you are at times unpredictable in your actions and words, but always reliable in your loving intentions.

And once that safety has been established, you'll be celebrated rather than shamed.

"Should you try to be consistent with your past self?
Should a newspaper try to be consistent with past news?"

— Derek Sivers

Without deviations, contradictions or inconsistencies, change can not occur.

And if change cannot occur, life cannot keep moving.

But life will always keep moving, no matter what.

Even in death, the body continues to change.

And its cells continue to live on inside the many animals and plants that aided in its decomposition.

So death does not stop life, and is not the opposite of life.

Death is merely life contradicting itself.

Are you contradicting yourself?

Great. That means you are living. Growing. Becoming more whole.

Allowing yourself to be inconsistent or contradictory doesn't make you less of a person.

It makes you more.

Now to be clear:

The fact you can be inconsistent and contradictory doesn't mean you should do so for the sake of it (unless that's what you want).

All I want is for you to know you have the power and freedom to do so.

Remember:

There is nothing that you have to do.

If you want to stay forever consistent with your current persona, why not?

You'll be consistently awesome!

The invitation is simply to observe your personality and witness how each aspect of it is working in your favor or not.

Maybe your identity as a tortured artist is working great when it comes to making good art and getting attention from teenage girls, but it's not working so great in terms of the emotional turmoil it creates for you.

Maybe that wall you built around your heart is protecting you from being hurt, but is also blocking you from being loved.

Most of our patterns aren't inherently bad or good.

But they have a nuanced impact that can be partly desirable and partly undesirable to you (a sentiment that can shift over time).

Most of your patterns have a purpose.

They are handcrafted spears, which were made for your survival.

The positive purpose of a pattern you believe is bad might be a competing commitment you haven't discovered yet.

Many of the patterns you think you're trying to change about yourself are actually patterns you're trying really hard to keep. But your mind's protecting you from seeing why.

When you find out why you cling to the pattern, and compare your competing commitments, you can reconcile them (as we learned in chapter 24) and dissolve them into love.

Remember:

Most of our unhelpful patterns at some point saved our sanity.

If it's still keeping you safe from something you're not ready to handle yet, don't force healing just because people say you should.

That said, if you find yourself wanting to liberate yourself from them, that might be exactly the direction in which you're naturally moving right now.

In the rest of this chapter we'll learn how to do so without using force or breaking our spears.

MYTH:

Comfort is the enemy of growth.

REALITY:

If you spend too much time in discomfort, you wear out.

Contrary to popular belief, growth happens within your comfort zone.

Growth happens from balancing cycles of comfort and discomfort.

Tension and release. Just like everything in nature.

Spending time at the edge of your comfort zone puts an increased load on your nervous system, which stimulates growth.

But it's returning to your comfort zone that gives you the nourishment to actually grow.

This is no different from building muscle in the gym.

Going to the gym doesn't build muscle. It tears it down.

It increases the demand for nourishment.

And what builds muscle is tending to that nourishment:

Sleeping, resting, hydrating and eating.

Building character is no different.

If you'd spend every day in the gym without proper rest or nutrition, all your muscles would atrophy.

If you'd spend every day out of your comfort zone, you wouldn't get growth but trauma.

In a tragic twist of events, your nervous system would get so used to discomfort and stress that these would become your new comfort zone.

And the biggest challenge would be to move to a state of calm.

This means that spending too much time out of your comfort zone would make comfort uncomfortable for you.

This makes it really hard to still give yourself the nourishment you need, because now everything is stress and nothing is recovery.

I'm not speculating here. I've actually been there.

Your comfort zone and your desire to grow can seem like competing commitments.

But like most competing commitments, they want the same thing for you expressed in different ways.

They are both expressions of love, trying to make you feel safe.

One by creating a safe environment, the other by making you more capable to feel okay in environments that aren't as safe.

When you find yourself acting on either of these commitments, it can be tempting to reject yourself:

"I shouldn't keep myself so comfortable, I should be doing crazy stuff!"

But that's just rowing against the stream.

Bungee jumping isn't an inherently better activity than binge-watching.

And as you know, whatever you feel like doing most is what you'll do anyway.

The only choices to make is whether you'll enjoy it fully, or spice it with self-hate.

Allow yourself to move at your natural rhythm and balance will take care of itself —as we saw in chapter 8.

—*"Out of your comfort zone is where the magic happens."*—

Yes, and...when you pay attention, the magic happens everywhere.

It's just that out of your comfort zone, you feel a surge of adrenaline, excitement or fear.

And what do all these have in common?

They heighten your awareness. Sharpen all your senses. Make you feel alive.

No wonder you'll notice the magic!

But that aliveness you feel after going on a roller coaster ride or jumping out of a plane?

It's always there. It's not going anywhere.

When you're wrapped in a fluffy blanket, sipping a warm cup of tea or laying in a soft hammock on a quiet beach, isn't that *"where the magic happens"* too?

Comfort zone, no comfort zone... the magic never leaves.

You can do the same thing twice and feel completely different about it.

There is no comfort zone.

Just you.

Responding to your surroundings with comfort or discomfort depending on your capacity in the moment.

Welcome things as they are (including how you feel about them), and the zone disappears.

Pick any trait you consider a defining part of your personality.

How do you know it's typical of you?

Because its opposite is not.

We know we are humble when we're not braggy.

We know we are flexible when we're not stubborn.

We know we are compassionate when we're not insensitive.

This can make it seem like personality traits are binary, an on/off switch of some sorts.

But every quality which your behavior can embody exists on a spectrum.

If you'd be 5% less compassionate, that still wouldn't make you insensitive. But you would indeed be 5% less compassionate.

Between each pair of opposing qualities, there is a rich world of subtle distinctions you can move between.

And there is no clear border at which you stop being one and become the other.

Everyone knows that extreme politeness isn't rude and that

extreme rudeness isn't polite. But in the murky middle regions, if you'd try to move slowly and gradually from politeness to rudeness, there'd be no exact point at which the politeness ends and the rudeness begins.

Every quality is inextricably tied to its opposite.

Without its opposite, the quality would cease to exist as a concept.

The character traits which seem to be defining qualities of your personality are actually just the positions you've become comfortable taking on their respective spectrum.

Please pardon me if this question comes across as impolite, but just how widely can you spread your legs? And how tightly can you close them?

The gap between these two is the range you have on the spectrum of spreading your legs.

If you look at the spectrum of any pair of qualities in your personality, you'll notice you have a certain range as well.

For example, let's take the spectrum of generosity and selfishness.

If your personality has a pattern of being more generous than selfish, you might see yourself as a generous person.

But this isn't really who you are, it's simply your standard position on this spectrum.

Walking around with your legs closed most of the time doesn't make you a closed-legged person. Your legs have range.

Behaving generously most of the time doesn't make you a generous person. Your generosity has range.

Exactly how generous can you allow yourself to be?

And how selfish can you allow yourself to be?

The gap between those two is the range of your generosity.

Your standard position on any spectrum can be locked or loose (which is of course a spectrum in itself, but let's not go too meta).

Imagine for example that the muscles in your legs, hips and lower back are all extremely tight and stiff.

Their standard position might still be the same one as the legs of a ballerina standing still.

But the ballerina's legs have a loose position —a wide range of movement. Whereas a person with stiff and tight muscles has a locked position. They can't do any kind of split. And when they try, it hurts.

The same applies to your personality's position on any given spectrum. Some of your positionalities are loose. Others are locked (the locked ones tend to have the catchphrase *"that's just how I am"*).

Let's take the example of someone's personality being positioned as left-wing on the political spectrum.

If this is a locked position, they will never be able to consider the value of a policy proposed by a right-wing politician. It'll seem wrong by default.

If this is a loose position, they will have a habit of thinking in left-wing perspectives, but will find themselves able to consider right-wing view points, and even to support some if they ever prove to be a better tool for the situation at hand.

Every positionality that is "locked" for you right now is simultaneously a strength and a weakness.

It is a strength because nobody can influence you into behaving opposite to it.

It is a weakness because if you ever needed to, you couldn't behave opposite to it.

Let's say your personality has a locked position on the spectrum of agreeableness.

This would mean you would find it impossible not to be agreeable in arguments, because *"that's just how you are."*

This agreeableness is a strength that can open many doors for you which would remain close to a disagreeable person.

But if someone is ever intent on crossing your boundaries, it can prove to be a weakness too.

And if you run into too many situations like that, you might start to see your pattern of agreeableness as a problem to get rid of.

But remember: There are no problems.

And it's better not to get rid of a useful tool in case you ever need it.

So what's the solution?

Create range instead of change.

People who *force* themselves to change their personality often end up in a new locked position that's the opposite of the previous one.

But this doesn't make much of a difference. Because that new locked position will be both a strength and a weakness, just like before.

Creating *range* instead of change means not erasing the strengths of your previous position(s) but incorporating them.

Creating range is allowing your personality to expand outward from how it is right now.

Instead of getting rid of your patterns, you transcend them.

Gaining the ability to open your legs real wide doesn't turn you into an open-legged person.

All it does is increase the amount of positions accessible to you.

(wink)

Similarly, gaining the ability to behave like a drama queen doesn't turn you into one.

It only increases the amount of emotional expressions accessible to you.

What would happen if you tried to be 5% more empathetic right now? Or 5% less?

Would you still be the same person?

I imagine you'd barely notice the difference.

What about 10%? Or 50%?

This is an explorative journey.

Look at it as personality yoga.

Take any trait that's typical for you and move into another position on the spectrum.

Hang out in that unusual position for a while.

Breathe.

How does it feel?

- ...painful?
- ...yummy?
- ...refreshing?

Can you imagine what it would look or feel like to still be the same person —but on the other side of this particular spectrum?

Would that be any different from still having the same body, but being able to do a full split (or bench twice your bodyweight)?

Stretching your stiff personality traits is to your psychology what stretching stiff muscles is to your physical health.

"One can only go as high as they have been low."

— David R. Hawkins

One surprising reason we'd all benefit from learning to express character traits opposite to the ones we think define us is that being able to access one extreme of the spectrum gives us access to a greater range on the other side as well.

This can sound counterintuitive, so let's examine.

To continue using the metaphor of the body:

Your body has a center of gravity, which is a point where your weight is balanced.

When you move or reach out in one direction, your center of gravity shifts.

If you stretch your arm far in front of you, that moves your center of gravity forward.

If nothing else would change, you would tip over because the balance is disrupted.

But notice how, when you actually try this, you don't fall.

Why is that? Your body instinctively adjusts.

It leans back slightly, shifts your hips backwards or finds another way to provide equal counterweight that helps balance the forward reach of your arms.

If for some reason your body wouldn't have enough range of motion to provide this counterweight, you'd fall on your face.

This is also the principle behind construction cranes.

The long arm of the crane can reach out to lift heavy loads.

However, cranes always need at least equal counterweight at the base, or they will fall on their face.

The heavier the load or the farther it reaches, the more counterweight is needed.

I "personally" believe the same principle applies to our personalities.

For example:

The greater the amount of selfishness you allow yourself to act with, the greater the amount of generosity you'll have access to.

If you can't set boundaries on your time, money and energy, you will often find yourself not having anything left to give to others.

But when you allow yourself to make more selfish choices, your cup is always full and can be generously shared.

Your selfishness is the counterweight for your generosity.

Similarly, if leadership is a locked part of your personality, you'll be a worse leader than a leader who also has access to followership as a counterweight.

Because as a leader who's great at following, you'll be able to make better decisions.

Like following the lead of people with more relevant expertise for the situation you find yourself in.

(As a side note: People with an incessant need to be in the "dominant position" are the most easily manipulable.

All it takes is one intelligent person who acts submissive and supplicant, while steering the "leader" towards certain decisions and giving their ego credit for it.)

"Father, forgive them; for they do not know what they are doing."

— Jesus Christ

The locked positionalities within our personalities are held hostage by our judgments and condemnations.

As long as we condemn a behavior in others, we'll have a hard time consciously accessing it ourselves.

But if we remember the example that learning to develop more selfishness can give you greater access to generosity, then condemning selfishness can decrease your access to generosity (so funnily enough, judging selfishness can make you more selfish).

That means the pathway to personal liberation is the pathway of forgiveness.

And what is forgiveness?

It's a way to "find" love in a game of hide and seek that would otherwise be lost.

A way to "win" the game no matter what.

When love's so well hidden that no one sees it, forgiveness is a way to tell others (or yourself) *"I am the love you thought was not here. And I am here for you, too."*

That is the essence of forgiveness.

The more qualities you can forgive in yourself and others, the more you can move through life freely, unburdened by the positionalities of your persona.

You can still embody all the same qualities you enjoy in yourself.

But rather than the behavior being locked in a state of neurosis, a loop you can't seem to move out of, it'll be a choice you made out of love. Your favorite out of the infinite ways to express your range.

The more strongly you tie your personality to any specific trait, the more you limit access to your inherent power and freedom because every locked trait is a part of you that can not move.

You may wonder: *"Why would we want to limit ourselves from being able to move?"*

We do so because we don't trust our ability to move across a certain spectrum in a safe and responsible way.

If there were no repercussions and you gave yourself full permission to be cruel to anyone, would you still trust yourself to be a kind person?

When the answer is no, many of us will keep our position on the cruelty to kindness spectrum locked in "kindness".

But as you may recall, when we don't have range of movement, we don't have counterweight.

So in reality, you can't be kind without the capacity for cruelty.

Kindness without the possibility of cruelty is impotence.

It's a leg that could not run if your life depended on it

(And just to be clear: Cruelty without the capacity for kindness is impotence too.

It's a leg that couldn't stop kicking if your life depended on it.)

In this sense, you can see any spectrum on which you have limited range as a spectrum in which you are still developing.

Children, who are still in early stages of development, are in many ways impotent too.

If young children get lost in the grocery store, they're not able to drive home by themselves.

So their parents will limit their permitted range of motion until they are mature and responsible enough to get home safely on their own accord.

A child is dependent on their parents for their sense of safety.

It's the limitations and boundaries set by the parents that give them their freedom.

Because without them, they'd often put themselves in danger.

A certain part of your personality can be in an early stage of development on its spectrum.

In that case, just like a child is dependent for its survival on the limitations set by its parents, you will be dependent on the limitations of the position you locked yourself in for yours.

Children naturally grow up.

And as they do so, good parents will gradually let go of the reins and permit their children a wider range of movement.

The same is true of your personality.

As you gain life experience, it will naturally grow and mature.

And just like a child being forced to grow up too fast will hinder its development more than it will benefit it, trying to force yourself into personal growth can hinder your personality's development.

If the desire for personal growth is present in you, that means the process has already started.

Now all you need to do is gradually let go of the reins and permit yourself a wider range of spontaneous movement.

And of course, as you'd do with any child, be patient and understanding.

But continue to keep an eye on them.

"Quit trying to change your life.
Instead, allow life to change you."

— Tej Dosa

Personality traits go through a four stage process of liberation.

Notice that in each of the stages we're about to discuss you are, in fact, equally free.

The freedom simply takes on different shapes depending on your awareness of it (and relationship to it).

Stage 1: Innocence (Infancy)

Freedom through ignorance.

In this stage, you have a full range of motion across the spectrum of the trait.

Because you are not yet aware of any potential dangers of spreading its fire in the world.

Stage 2: Shame (Childhood)

Freedom through limitation.

As you get burned from playing with more personality fire than you can handle, you learn to keep yourself safe by limiting the range of the trait you allow yourself to play with.

Controlling the range of the trait's fire allows you to continue freely engaging with the world in a safe way.

Stage 3: Rebellion (Adolescence)

Freedom through polarization.

In this stage, you feel drawn to experiment with positions on the spectrum which are opposite to the ones you've previously shamed yourself into.

You play with edges and test limits in ways that don't always benefit you or those around you in the short term (but benefit your mastery of the trait's spectrum in the long term).

You are playing with the fire of this trait and learning through experience how it can bring light and destruction depending on how it's used.

Stage 4: Sovereignty (Adulthood)

Freedom through responsibility.

Now that you have liberated the full range of the trait, you can become de-liberate with it.

You know that all positions on the spectrum are available to you. But you choose the ones that most honor the integrity of yourself *and* others.

You know the power of the trait's fire and you have mastered it.

The fire can continue to burn safely because you know exactly how to guide it.

Most self-development advice gets stuck in the adolescence phase.

It'll say things like *"Your negative thoughts aren't working for you, so you must always think positively."*

Which keeps you locked in a positive position (making you negative about negativity, because without that counterweight, you would fall on your face).

It'll tell you:

"Stop being such a good guy or good girl, because it's ruining your dating life."

Which then locks you in the position of the jerk or the "boss-bitch", ruining your dating life in opposite ways.

A great example of why you're better off creating range than change.

It'll say:

"Your life is short, so you must not let a second of it go to waste."

Which locks you in a position of activity and accounting, leading you to waste many precious seconds hustling and grinding when you need to rest (or would've enjoyed something else) and lose lots of time fretting over "lost time".

By allowing yourself to be liberated from a locked position in your personality, you gain the ability to choose.

You move the trait from adolescence into adulthood.

—*"Can I embody both sides of this spectrum and still be me?"*—

The answer, of course, is always *"Yes, why wouldn't you?"*

With each locked position you liberate, you acknowledge that this trait did not define you.

You acknowledge that the idea that "being that way" is a requirement for being you, is an illusion.

And as you increase your range, your identity gets smaller and smaller. While you get bigger and bigger.

No longer a slave to your own personality but not having lost it either, you are free.

You can do the same thing you've always done. But you now know that you could do the complete opposite if you wanted to.

You've experienced range instead of change.

And have transcended the illusion of self-development.

(...Oh, and just in case I wasn't clear about that:

You are under no obligation to increase your range in any way unless you want to.

Embrace yourself as you are. I'm only here to share perspectives to explore.)

If you would stop pursuing any personal growth at all, the growth would still happen.

How did your grandparents earn their wisdom?

Simple, life gave it to them. Through many games of hide and seek.

Every trait in your personality will mature at its own pace if you allow it to and refrain from meddling too much.

Some patterns will gently dissolve. Others will play themselves out until they're tired of doing so.

There are plenty of lessons I refused to learn until I hit rock bottom with them.

Would I have still learned them without that? Who knows.

There's no point in wondering because that's not what happened.

But after witnessing myself for quite some time, I've become convinced that when you leave any pattern alone for long enough without losing track of it, it'll eventually either gracefully grow up, or break itself so painfully that it has no other choice.

So once again, it seems to me like you can't do it wrong.

But you *can* make it easier or harder, depending on how willingly you allow life to happen through you.

"An authentically powered person lives in love.
Love is the energy of the soul.
Love is what heals the personality.
There is nothing that cannot be healed by love."

— Gary Zukav

Whenever you find yourself stuck in an unpleasant position or pattern, love is the force that will liberate you.

Forgiveness can be a way to bring love to any pattern you had demonized inside yourself.

And the two processes we've just discussed are no different:

By not interfering and allowing growth to arrive at its own pace, you are energetically saying *"I embrace myself as I am right now."*

And once again, you've found love without making an effort to.

By letting an unhelpful pattern play out until you hit rock bottom with it, love is invited in.

Not just because the pattern is embraced, but also because you reach a point where the pattern becomes so painful, you find yourself thinking *"enough is enough."*

And that's when you've found the hiding place of love. Enough is enough because you love yourself and you want to treat yourself better.

Another way to bring love to a pattern or a trait you feel "stuck on" is holding it in non-judgmental, non-expecting awareness.

You just watch it without wishing it away.

Yes, it is true that this can make the pattern dissolve.

But as long as that's your goal, I can guarantee you it won't.

Because love given with the intent to make something leave will only make it want to stay.

Love doesn't play anyone else's games.

The standard paradigm of personal development re-affirms the idea that you need to change.

But personal liberation can only occur when you allow yourself to be free not to do so.

Personal liberation starts happening when you're no longer telling yourself you should be anything more than you are.

But instead recognize that there will always be more to you to explore.

And honor how much of that exploration you have capacity for right now.

Either way, you'll grow at the same pace:

The pace it happens at.

While you're busy doing what you want.

And occasionally pretending not to because you love hide and seek.

CHAPTER 30
LET'S MAKE LOVE

The best way to find love is to make it.

Love is made through repetitive, rhythmic motions.

In and out.

An endless dance of hiding and seeking.

Of welcoming and releasing.

A game everything in existence is playing at all times.

Each at its own unique pace. All moving to the same rhythm.

You are never not making love.

So perhaps instead of saying *"the best way to find love is to make it"*, it would be more accurate to say *"the best way to find love is to realize you're already making it."*

Every time you breathe in, you *welcome* air into your lungs.

It is found.

Every time you breathe out, you *release* air back into the world.

"Time for another round!"

Can you pay attention to these rhythms of welcoming and releasing?

Can you become aware of the love you're making?

Any time you welcome anything, whether it is a feeling, a personality trait or another person, you receive the unique flavor of love hidden inside it.

And any time you release it, you give it the opportunity to go hide again.

So that if it wants to, it can give you another chance to delight in wondering where it went and seeing it appear again

Can you allow yourself to enjoy this as much as a kid enjoys a game of peek-a-boo?

(I don't think it's a coincidence they do.)

To welcome something fully, you must also welcome its opposite. Otherwise it can't exist.

Remember, we can only identify something when we can point out both sides of its spectrum:

"It is this, because it is not that."

This is why clinging on to a certain outcome tends to result in not getting it.

If we don't allow its opposite to be a possibility, we don't allow the thing we want to be a possibility either.

In an abstract sense, releasing and welcoming are one and the same.

When we welcome one side of a spectrum but refuse to welcome its opposite the spectrum stops existing for us.

To welcome a thing's opposite, we must first release our holding from it.

Because clasped hands can't receive anything.

To welcome the night, we must release our attachment to the day.

To welcome the day, we must release our attachment to the night.

Whenever we release something, we welcome its opposite automatically.

It is one movement.

Whenever you release, you welcome.

But a thing can only be fully welcomed by welcoming its opposite too.

Because if we don't allow the night to come, there will never be another day.

By welcoming both a thing and its opposite, we make love to the distinction that creates its existence. And honor its place as a part of the greater whole.

By allowing it to go in and out of existence, we make the love that gives birth to it.

Every feeling, sensation, thought or experience that could potentially exist within you can only come to exist because of two opposing qualities being allowed to make love through you.

So the more traits you allow yourself to embody without losing your sense of self, the more feelings you allow yourself to feel and the more ways you allow yourself to be, the more you become a space of nothingness.

A space of pure potential, a free and powerful vessel through which anything can be brought into this life.

That is how you *"maximize your potential"*.

Not by forcing yourself to live up to some narrow standard of perfection set by the current zeitgeist. But by becoming an embodiment of potential itself.

To find love, focus your undivided attention on anything (or anyone) long enough until you either find the love within or discover the love that is inherent in your own attention.

I never realized it while it was being written, but there is not a word in this book that isn't about making love.

Making love is having a goal or desire, climbing to its peak and then beginning the cycle all over again.

Making love is releasing your motivation, wondering where it went, and realizing it never left.

Making love is feeling like you must get rid of a problem, then realizing it was never there.

Making love is faking it, then realizing that's not helping you one bit.

Making love is feeling vulnerable and inadequate, then discovering that's what true confidence is.

Making love is giving your power away, then reclaiming it.

Making love is following what brings joy, and moving away from what doesn't.

Making love is bringing joy to things that at first felt uncomfortable or hard.

Making love is allowing your nature to move you.

Making love is your real priorities being shamelessly revealed.

Making love is dying and being born again.

Making love is discovering you had already decided but didn't know it.

Making love is making up a whole bunch of excuses for your actions, then re-claiming your sovereignty by admitting it was just what you wanted to do deep down.

Making love is having milkshakes, eating marshmallows *and* making millions, even when adults say you have to choose.

Making love is balancing short-term and long-term satisfaction.

Making love is admitting you can't resist.

Making love is spending a lifetime tasting every different flavor and realizing they all have something to offer.

Making love is showing up in drag and being so immersed in the role that you forget who you are.

Making love is joining in endless games of hide and seek.

Making love is opening and closing to the feelings inside.

Making love is commanding someone to lead you but knowing you are still in control.

Making love is allowing yourself to be restrained and finding freedom in it.

Making love is living your purpose without even knowing it.

Making love is commitment. And sometimes confusion about that.

Making love is discovering what you want by doing it.

Making love is a whole lot of "YES!!!" and respecting the importance of your "NO!".

Making love is always remembering where you are on the slippery staircase of morality.

Making love is recognizing the devil inside you and still choosing goodness.

Making love is realizing you are not your personality. But a powerful being who can welcome and release any trait and bring it into being by embodying it.

Making love is welcoming and releasing but also being welcomed and released.

Reclaiming your life by letting it claim you.

And realizing it's all one.

CHAPTER 31
BUT... IT'S NOT THAT SIMPLE!

"Sink into what you are right now.

Just be that thing. Stop resisting.

Exactly where you are right now is perfect.

And that's a hard truth to grasp.

Because you right away, you think 'yeah, well what about _____ ???'"

— **Duncan Trusseel**

One thing about this book which I imagine some people might feel annoyed with is that the underlying message of every chapter is basically:

"Everything's alright. Don't worry about it. Just allow yourself to live and make love."

If such a message has you exclaiming *"But... It's not that. Simple!"*, then you may be right.

We can spend a lifetime learning to put this into practice (or multiple lifetimes, depending on who you ask).

The heart of the journey is accepting yourself as you are and accepting the way life is expressing itself through you.

Which includes patiently accepting where you currently do not find the capacity to accept yourself yet.

Everyone's doing the best they can, including you and I.

We can aspire to do" better" in some regard.

But if we can't do "better" right now, then the soonest we can do "better" (whatever that means) is the moment after this one.

And if we manage to do so in that next moment, then the aspiration we felt in this moment was already the beginning of that.

So whatever you think would be a better version of you is already who you are right now.

Waiting to be welcomed and released by accepting yourself in your present way of being.

This is truly all there is to be done.

Because it's impossible to be any other way than you are.

If after reading this book, you throw all your self-imposed self-development habits out the window, then that's because you wanted to.

If you continue living exactly the way you were living, then that's because you wanted to

Both are you being as you are.

"Effort less" doesn't necessarily mean "do less".

It means allowing life to live through you with as little forcing as possible, rather than expending lots of energy to maintain the illusion that you're in control.

You will indeed always do what you want.

Whether you do it effortlessly or forcefully.

But ask yourself:

Who's doing this wanting?

Where does your wanting come from?

Are you in control of what you want?

Or is the "wanting" in itself the way that life is moving you? The way the ocean is shaping your wave?

There is nothing to be done.

Because even if you were to do something.

It was already done for you.

"And now that you don't have to be perfect, you can be good."

— John Steinbeck

The paradox of self-development is that the same process through which it empowers and liberates us is also the process through which it perpetuates neurosis, creates hamster wheel routines and makes us feel like there's always a next thing to fix.

This book has a paradoxical message too.

Because it tells you that you are 100% free.

Yet it implies that all effort to do something other than what you were already going to do is futile and you should just let life happen through you.

It says you have all the power.

Yet it can be interpreted as saying you're never truly making any decisions because you'll always be doing what you want most deep down, whether you think so or not.

But as with all of life's paradoxes:

Once you get the joke, you may find it's all one.

A whole lotta love,

Pep

ABOUT THE AUTHOR AND THIS BOOK

Let's get this secret out in the open first:

Yes, it's the author writing this chapter.

And he finds himself wondering how many writers secretly toot their own horn at the end of a book, referring to themselves in third person.

He also finds it quite cumbersome and mildly uncomfortable to do so.

So he hereby decides to switch back to speaking with you directly.

Since this is a book for you, and not a biography to convince you how awesome I am (though I do think I am), I'll keep the personal details in this chapter concise.

My first games of hide and seek started out in hard mode.

Childhood abuse. Teenage depression. Chronic anxiety keeping me from sleep as an adolescent.

If I could travel back in time and give my younger self this book, he'd probably scoff at it. And call me ignorant for even insinuating the possible presence of love.

But then again: That's exactly what he was supposed to be doing at that time.

How else could he ever have learned the lessons that would lead to writing this?

And what he did have in common with me was a deep commitment to authenticity and connection.

I realized early on that the standard roadmap presented by society didn't work for me.

Whether it was about relationships, work, health or lifestyle, I always knew something more aligned existed —and that following the paved path wouldn't get me there.

So I dropped out of high school to self-educate through full time explorimentation.

I spent over fifteen years experiencing, exploring, experimenting, practicing and playing with the edges of social and personal reality.

Every day, I'd go on the street, talk to people of all walks of life and embark on spontaneous adventures.

I followed what excited me with ruthless commitment. Even if it led to negative experiences.

This is where the themes of "inescapability" and "you can't do it wrong" come from in this book.

Looking back, even though I was never aware of it, I've always done exactly what was needed to lead me here.

They often seemed like terrible choices.

But with the hindsight of a thirty-three year old, I'm amazed by how they were beneficial in ways impossible to predict.

When after a decade of depression I finally woke up happy, I was shocked.

"Holy fudge! Is this what other people feel all the time?"

It wasn't. Turns out many people struggle with dissatisfaction.

But I had been too focused on myself to notice. That's how it goes when love is hiding.

So I started sharing the fruits of my exploriments with others wherever they could be of service.

Eventually, various people kept pushing me to start a blog.

Which I did. And much to my surprise, I quite liked it.

This coincided with the peak of self-help culture in the 2010s.

And my stories would often resonate with people looking for unique perspectives on these topics.

Whenever my advice or ideas were helpful to them, readers would send me tips and thank you notes in return.

The largest tip I received was exactly one thousand euros.

It was a sign that this modest blog could really go somewhere.

But right in that same period, something dawned on that crippled my confidence as a writer and stopped me from posting:

Most of the personal growth advice I was sharing could make 2 opposing impacts, depending on the reader.

While for 1 person, it might be exactly what they need to hear to find happiness.

For someone else, it could reinforce the idea that they're broken and need fixing.

And there was no way for me to control this.

Meanwhile, in my personal life, I was about to have my own experience with this in an unexpected way.

"You can't hate yourself into becoming someone you love."

— Ikara

After years of focusing on personal growth, I had created a perfect life that was pretty much running on autopilot.

Peak health. Peak performance. Peak positive emotions.

Making money from anywhere in the world.

And to top it all off, I was swept up in the magical rapture of young love.

Then one day, I got a phone call that my Dad was in the hospital.

The next few weeks flew by quite fast.

And there were a lot of beautiful moments within our family.

Perhaps it brought us closer than we'd ever been.

Because when he passed, a lot of love that had been hidden was made explicit.

That was one of the first hints for me, that there's love to be found in even the worst experiences.

But eventually, I became overwhelmed with grief.

I found myself unable to perform at the level I was used to, or show up with the same positive energy.

And what I discovered shocked me:

My perfect life and healthy habits were actually an addiction. Just like the many others I had overcome.

Sure, going to the gym is better than getting drunk at midday.

But that doesn't mean the underlying mechanism isn't the same:

Whenever I couldn't do all these things that were so good for me, my self-worth tanked.

There I was, living a life way beyond what my younger self would have considered paradise.

But if for one short period, I couldn't perform up to my own standards, I felt ashamed of who I was.

That experience was a true blessing.

Because it gave me the opportunity to learn to love myself at my worst.

And a lot of what stopped me from doing so, were deeply ingrained beliefs I had picked up from the world of self-development:

- *"When you feel bad, you should push through and do the thing anyway."*
- *"Negative people, thoughts or feelings should be avoided at all costs."*
- *"We should always be the best version of ourselves."*

I got the opportunity to experience the exact thing I worried about when I had quit writing:

The destructive side of positive beliefs.

Now luckily, I had also experienced the destructive power of negative beliefs earlier in life.

So it was clear that the answer wasn't to rebel against the beliefs I had picked up in the self-help space.

I had to wait and allow life to teach me a perspective that could reconcile them with what I was going through now.

The amount of chaos and challenges I was met with only increased in the years after.

But it served to bring me to a place where even when I'm not at my best, I no longer feel bad about myself.

And even when an emotion I experience is not pleasant, the undercurrent of happiness is very much present.

From the outside, it could look like I was "doing better" when I was twenty nine.

But internally, I wouldn't wanna be anywhere else in life than I am today.

It actually feels like living *more*, not less.

Many who think they are seeking self-development are really seeking self-acceptance.

There's a hidden neuroticism to the self-help industry.

A sense of inflated self-importance, while simultaneously reinforcing the idea that you're a never-ending project in need of fixing.

And the former serves to make sure we never find out the latter is happening.

Because whether the belief is installed intentionally or not:

People who think they always need 1 more fix, are the best customers.

Drug dealers know this. And do many marketers in the self-help industry.

And just like with some drugs: if consuming the product makes you feel great about yourself for a while, you may not realize that it's harming you.

Like the high of cocaine, the confidence gained from self improvement can be volatile.

There's nothing wrong with losing twenty pounds and feeling better because of it.

Being in healthy shape is universally a good thing.

As is writing a gratitude journal.

Or learning to regulate your emotions.

The subtle difference I'm talking about here is:

Can you still be happy and feel good about yourself without it?

Or is it something that distracts you from the untended wounds you have?

If you're working hard to become a better version of yourself but struggling with resistance, ask yourself:

Is it 100% true that I intrinsically want to be this new person? That this new version of me inspires me for its own sake?

Or is it that I want to feel loved, happy and safe?

And that I believe this new "improved" version of me would be more worthy or capable of having that?

The latter would explain why you are feeling so much resistance.

Because telling yourself you should be better than you are is giving yourself the opposite of what you are trying to achieve with this whole project.

So there's wisdom in the resistance when you dare to embrace it.

Trust its message. Force yourself a bit less. Sink into what you are.

Observe what happens when you do.

You might just find out that the best version of yourself you could possibly be is you.

The paradox is that even for self-development purposes, embracing yourself and the flow of life is still a better approach.

Because if you have unrecognized neuroses, attempts to fix yourself might only reinforce them.

In contrast, embracing yourself as you are is an act of becoming the love and safety you've been craving.

I wrote this book by accident.

I was trying really hard to write another book.

But while I was procrastinating on that, this one wrote itself.

A question that crossed my mind frequently was:

Why write another book about personal growth?

Not only is the world already full of them, it's no longer even the focus of my own work.

In recent years, I've been facilitating workshops on interpersonal practices, like Authentic Relating and Circling.

And in our personal life, Ari and I have been hosting events with a similar purpose: To bring people together and get them to connect more deeply.

These are all relational practices. Yet there I go, writing another book focused on the individual.

But while the words poured onto this paper —or more accurately, this computer screen— their purpose dawned on me.

This is a book that aims to liberate.

That hopes to help you transcend the need for forceful self-development.

Because your personality, and the wholeness of your heart, aren't projects to be finished.

They're treasures to be discovered over a lifetime.

Doesn't matter at which pace or through which method you find love each time.

You are as you are. There is need to change anything.

Yet you are free to change anything you want.

When we let this realization sink in on a cellular level —that we can welcome ourselves exactly as we are— our self-obsession fades.

And as a result, all that attention and energy we used to spend on it is freed up.

Because when you being you no longer requires effort.

You get to be here, effortlessly.

With attention and energy to spare.

Allowing you to truly connect with the others that surround you.

But who knows?

Maybe that's a topic for another book.

If any part of this book resonated with you, I'd love to be in touch. You can find me on:

X: @peptalksblog

Instagram: @peptalksblog

Website / blog: peptalksblog.com

Hold on... One more thing before we part ways.

Can I ask you a quick favor?

This is the first edition of this book, and you are one of the very first people to read it.

Naturally, that means three things:

1. I'm extremely curious about how this book resonated with you.

2. There's an opportunity for this book to reach even more people.

3. There are undoubtedly ways this book could be improved.

If you could find it in your heart to help me, here are three simple ways you could make a huge difference:

1. **Share what impacted you most.**

   If there's a passage that you highlighted or found deeply meaningful, I'd love to hear about it. You can send me a private message or share it on social media (and tag me). The latter also spreads the word about this book.

2. **Let me know what was unclear.**

   If there's a section that felt confusing or left you scratching your head, your feedback would mean the world. It might signal where I can clarify or refine the text.

3. **Tell me what left you wanting more.**

   If something sparked your curiosity or left you yearning to explore a topic more deeply, let me know. When I see recurring themes, I can expand the chapter in future editions or explore the topic in a blog post.

Whether you choose to share your thoughts or not, I'm grateful for your time and attention.

Your willingness to journey with me through these ideas means more than I can say.

May you always find truth in the context of love.

Till we meet again,

Pep

Printed in Great Britain
by Amazon

57692525R00219